starts with an A

CREATIVE
TYPE

A Sourcebook of Classic and Contemporary Letterforms

Cees W. de Jong

Alston W. Purvis

Friedrich Friedl

CREATIVE TYPE

Thames & Hudson

'I JUST THINK OF A LETTER AND MARK AROUND IT.'

Frederic Goudy

Contents

ITC Franklin, 2004
David Berlow

Demos, 2004
Gerard Unger

Zapfino, 2003
Hermann Zapf

Kosmik, 2002
Erik van Blokland

Sabon Next, 2002
Jean François Porchez

Le Monde, 1997
Jean François Porchez

Linotype Syntax, 2000
Hans Eduard Meier

Aroma, 1999
Tim Ahrens

Gianotten, 1999
Antonio Pace

Markin, 1999
Alfred Tilp

Scarborough, 1998
Akira Kobayashi

Silvermoon, 1998
Akira Kobayashi

Atomatic, 1997
Johannes Plass

Finnegan, 1997
Jürgen Weltin

Spitz, 1997
Oliver Brentzel

Carumba, 1996
Jill Bell

Filosofia, 1996
Zuzana Licko

Tagliatelle, 1996
Alessio Leonardi

LinoLetter, 1992
Linotype

Linotype Didot, 1991
Linotype

Veto, 1994
Marco Ganz

Sho, 1992
Karlgeorg Hoefer

PMN Caecilia, 1990
Peter Matthias Noordzij

Officina, 1990
Erik Spiekermann

Industria, 1989
Neville Brody

Avenir, 1988
Adrian Frutiger

Frutiger Next, 2001
Adrian Frutiger

Stone, 1987
Sumner Stone

Lucida Sans, 1985
Kris Holmes/Charles Bigelow

Optima nova, 2002
Hermann Zapf

Accessible and easy to use, this very handy reference book for young designers provides a visual record of typeface evolution since 1985 and also has a section devoted to the modern classics of our age. Illustrations show the typefaces in use, sketches by the designers, first proofs, poster samples and whole type families. What you see, you can also get: all the original fonts, plus new and revised versions from the last ten to fifteen years, are available for purchase. The book also highlights the significant relationship between classic and contemporary typography.

I am a great fan of other professional 'typographers', such as the house painter, the carpenter and all those designing craftsmen who are almost impossible to pigeonhole. They produce an abundance of free, unconstrained applications; applications of an often very individual character and beauty, which determine our daily streetscape and, therefore, also our world.

I would like to thank Alston Purvis, Friedrich Friedl, Gerard Unger, Hermann Zapf, Erik van Blokland, Just van Rossum, Jean François Porchez, Hans Eduard Meier, Tim Ahrens, Antonio Pace, Alfred Tilp, Akira Kobayashi, Johannes Plass, Jürgen Weltin, Oliver Brentzel, Jill Bell, Zuzana Licko, Alessio Leonardi, Marco Ganz, Karlgeorg Hoefer, David Berlow, Peter Matthias Noordzij, Erik Spiekermann, Neville Brody, Adrian Frutiger, Sumner Stone, Charles Bigelow, Kris Holmes, Simone Wolf and in particular Otmar Hoefer.

In a world bombarded with communication, I hope this book will help us to find our way.

Cees W. de Jong, Laren, 2005

FERENCE au PAVILLON
PULAIRE le VENDREDI 4 MAI
par RENE LEVY.
SUR
VERITABLE GUERISON, CAUSE
FONDE DE LA MALADIE PHYSIQUE ET MENTALE
Lévy depuis 20 ans se consacre à la
 d'un MODE de VIE SIMPLE et PRATIQUE
découvrira la CLEF qui ouvre la porte
BONHEUR et de la SANTÉ

LIBRE

au 20 Mai
17 h avec :
EDJIAN,

Professional Typographers

In Demos there is relatively little difference between thick vertical and thin horizontal parts, which facilitates linear enlargement and reduction because it makes type in small sizes less prone to distortion.
Gerard Unger

A font is a software instruction to a printer to perform a task.
Erik van Blokland,
Just van Rossum

A revival of a revival was a double challenge: to try to discern Jan Tschichold´s own wishes for the original Sabon; and also to interpret the complexity of the original design, which was made in two versions for different systems.
Jean François Porchez

Barbedor is based on the written humanistic book scripts of the 15th century and its figures are those of broad-tipped pen writing. Tiny serif-like elements reveal the line of the writing utensil and emphasize the style of this typeface.
Hans Eduard Meier

I did not want Aroma to be one of those odourless and tasteless typefaces that sacrifice a natural feeling and neutralize the characteristic shapes of the letters.
Tim Ahrens

Rigorous design and the organic, unadorned construction of the individual characters give Linotype Gianotten a contemporary, highly readable appearance.
Antonio Pace

Atomatic seems to mirror the fast pace and technology of modern times. The slight lean to the right gives the impression of speed and movement.
Johannes Plass

Markin is named after the writing utensil with which it looks like it is drawn: the marker pen. Its even strokes display characteristics similar to those of a sans-serif typeface, but the stroke endings, with their typical handwritten look, give Markin a personal touch.
Alfred Tilp

Finnegan is a modern text font with its roots in the humanistic Old Face design. Its harmonic proportions make it extremely legible and particularly suitable for longer texts.
Jürgen Weltin

I borrowed my own handwriting for ITC Scarborough, a narrow, slightly slanted display face with many roman letterforms (especially in the capital letters), but with the overall style and flourishes of a cursive.
Akira Kobayashi

The motif of the Chrysler building symbolizes for me the language of form, which is also the basis for the Spitz font. A combination of pointed and semicircular elements develop their own aesthetic value through their interplay.
Oliver Brentzel

My fonts were created with a traditional broad-edged calligraphy pen, a pointed copperplate pen, a dry-bristle brush, a pointed Chinese brush, a Sharpie and even, in the case of Smack, the wrong end of a brush. Later, they were digitized and refined.

Jill Bell

Filosofia is my interpretation of a Bodoni. It shows my personal preference for a geometric Bodoni, while still incorporating such features as the slightly bulging round serif endings that often appeared in printed samples of Bodoni's work and reflect Bodoni's origins in letterpress technology.

Zuzana Licko

The techno sound of the 1990s, a personal computer, font creation software and a little innovation were the sources of the Tagliatelle font series.

Alessio Leonardi

Veto was the product of a desire to design an innovative sans-serif face. Starting with single letter-forms, I tried to leave out everything that seemed old-fashioned or superfluous.

Marco Ganz

Sho distinguishes itself in the extreme contrast between its strokes. A unique characteristic of the font is the way it uses simple round forms in some of its letters, giving a peppy and playful feel.

Karlgeorg Hoefer

The font Caecilia is recognizable by the completeness of each of its cuts. Each cut comes with small caps and Old Style figures, such details giving designers finer control over their own creations.

Peter Matthias Noordzij

Jeannette
Papiers Peints
SO
FRANÇOISE
KOFFIEHUIS
„Jennifer"
SHIRLE
FRANS
SHI

Officina embodies the ideals of efficient office
communication in its serif and sans-serif forms.
Its style is like that found on a traditional
typewriter, but altered to suit technological
developments. Both serif and sans-serif forms
are designed and spaced to offer optimal legibility.
Erik Spiekermann

The Stone family
consists of three types
of fonts: a serif, a
sans serif and an
informal style. Stone
fonts are very legible
and make a modern,
dynamic impression.
Sumner Stone

Insignia has the basic forms of
constructed Grotesque fonts and was
influenced by the New Typography of
the Bauhaus during the 1930s.
Neville Brody

The expansion and
harmonization of the
Frutiger palette has
allowed a much wider
range of uses. Now each
regular typeface has a
companion italic. The
areas of application are
almost limitless with the
reworked forms, and
Frutiger Next can be used
for anything from office
communications to
multimedia to complex
printed materials.
Adrian Frutiger

Zapfino fonts consist of four basic
alphabets with many additional
stylistic alternates, which can be
freely mixed to emulate the
variations in handwritten text.
Hermann Zapf

Type etc....

A small selection of visual images on type design and letterproofs: from lead letters, output on paper and film, to PostScript fonts and from News Gothic via Golden Type, Clarendon, Peignot and Beowolf to Syntax Antiqua.

Examples of News Gothic produced by
the American Type Founders, 1912.

REMIND

72 Point   5 A

STRANGE

60 Point   6 A

NEIGHBORS

48 Point   9 A

STRONG HOUSE

36 Point   10 A

BEAUTIFUL DESIGN

30 Point   15 A

PROMOTION DESERVED

24 Point   21 A

USING PERSUASIVE METHODS

18 Point   30 A

CONDENSED PUBLICATION HEADING

14 Point   35 A

MUCH PRINTED LITERATURE DISTRIBUTED

12 Point   40 A

PROMINENT CLERGYMEN ATTEND CONVENTION

10 Point   45 A

IMPORTANT MANUFACTURING CORPORATION PROSPERS

8 Point   42 A

LARGEST PUBLISHERS RECEIVING ATTRACTIVE BEFORE FOR SPACE

6 Point   40 A

CHARACTERS IN COMPLETE FONT

A B C D E F G H I J
K L M N O P Q R S
T U V W X Y Z & $
1 2 3 4 5 6 7 8 9 0
. . - ' : , ! ?

EXTRAORDINARY ENGAGEMENT OF THE FAMOUS

RIGA STOCK COMPANY

WONDERFUL SHAKESPEAREAN TRAGEDY

THE MERCHANT OF VENICE

WITH MARGUERITE SCARBOROUGH, EUGENE DAVIES
AND OTHER DISTINGUISHED ARTISTS

SYMPHONY ORCHESTRA DIRECTED BY JAMES RIGARDO

ACADEMY OF MUSIC, SOUTH BIRMINGHAM

WEEK BEGINNING MONDAY, MARCH SIXTH

LARGER CIRCULATION THAN ANY OTHER
MORNING NEWSPAPER IN THE COUNTY

The Mor

VOL. XXVII. No. 8142   WEEHAWKEN, N. J., MONDAY, JUNE

RICH CROP EXPECTED

**GENERAL BUYING OF WHEAT RESPONSIBLE FOR TREMENDOUS RISE
RECENTLY PREDICTED FOR STOCK MARKET VALUES**

EXPORTERS OFFERING UNUSUAL PRICES FOR DOMESTIC WHEAT CONSIGNED TO LOCAL MARKET

MILWAUKEE, June 1.—Encouraging reports from wheat growers are considered responsible for the activity among the larger buyers in all parts of the country. These buyers found the market heavily oversold, a condition which brought about the present shortage.

There seems to be little doubt that winter wheat crops will prove satisfactory owing to the lovely weather prevailing, and many of the western buyers show a tendency to hold their orders until the market becomes more settled. In some quarters there is a marked impression that the wheat market will soon become better, but until there is an increase in the buying no sustained change is looked for, and prices will remain as they are.

The bulk of the business is being done by local merchants who are constantly in touch with conditions of the market, which fact is responsible for their present activity.

Chicago operators recently sold more than 150,000 bushels to mills and a large quantity to exporters, although many large operators declare the demand was generally slow, and call attention to the fact that June was just one cent lower than July.

Coarse grains are reported to be in need of rain badly in many sections of the West, and the outlook for oats is not so very promising

Continued on Page Three

REWARD HEROES

**LOCAL FIREMEN RECEIVE GOLD MEDALS
FOR BRAVERY AND EFFICIENCY**

MAYOR LAUDS ENTIRE VOLUNTEER FIRE DEPARTMENT

Seven men received medals for valor from Mayor Hart at the ceremonies attending the unveiling of the Firemen's Monument in the city park yesterday. He congratulated them and the entire department on the excellent service they have rendered. The Mayor also took this occasion to compliment the Chief and his staff for the splendid appearance of the men, and the efficient manner in which

POLO TOURNAMENT ATTRACTS LARGE CROWDS

The polo tournament held annually at the Hendison Country Club continues to interest the summer colonists, who attend the games daily and display great enthusiasm.

Four more teams will compete to-morrow for the opportunity to play in the finals for a loving cup offered by the club.

**A MOST INTERESTING STORY
IN FOUR INSTALLMENTS**

Everyone should read THE BEATER, *a story of love by Jerome Havafis, which will appear daily, beginning with the Tuesday issue.*

THIS LINE IS COMPOSED IN HANDSOME   AMERICAN MUSEUM

EXPERTS
GOLF CO

WONDERFUL SCORE
IN CHAMPIONS

NEW YORK, June
Junior championship
new links of the Win
at Mineola. There wa
record on the first da
final round were play

The conditions dem
qualifying test the af
second rounds taking
several new traps an
added, this big handi
courses in the county

ORDERS BIG

RAILROADS PLACE ORD
COSTING SEVERAL

CONTEMPLATED ACTION GREET
STOCKHOLDERS, WHO SEEK
VOTE TO EMPOWER TH

The directors of se
railroad are consideri
renewing the big rail
rolling stock.

It is proposed to is
the purpose. Thousan
interest at three rate
will be convertible in
common stock and to
preferred stock, with
on the common stock
with debentures, and
price of 125 per cent

Those who contem
the improved earnin
and prove that many
whoever makes plain

Le Monde is a set of four highly legible fonts designed by Jean François Porchez for four specific applications in the French newspaper *Le Monde*.

'Le journal c'est un monsieur'. Jill Bell's Carumba is 'fun and funky', an expressive, contemporary letter full of South American passion and written with a calligraphy pen, a Chinese brush and the wrong end of a small brush.

Antonio Pace's Gianotten is the new, elegant letter for the city of Milan, created to present to the world this city of fashion, design and culture.

In almost no other field has the boom in technological advancement over the past few decades been as enormous as in the world of graphic design. The advent of the digital era has also entirely transformed this world. The appearance of the printed word has changed dramatically over the course of the years and has now been expanded to encompass the 'digital word'. Obviously, this has also been reflected in the process of letter design; from handwritten letters, via lead blocks, photolithography and Letraset, we have arrived in the PostScript and OpenType era. Now, an enormous degree of freedom and flexibility is being created with all kinds of hitherto undreamed of options.

Globalization has generated a cultural mix and a worldwide exchange of ideas, but, at the same time, nostalgia has played a key role. However, the tried and trusted principles of typography remain constant, such as the preconditions determined by form and rhythm, the relationship between black and white and shape against shape.

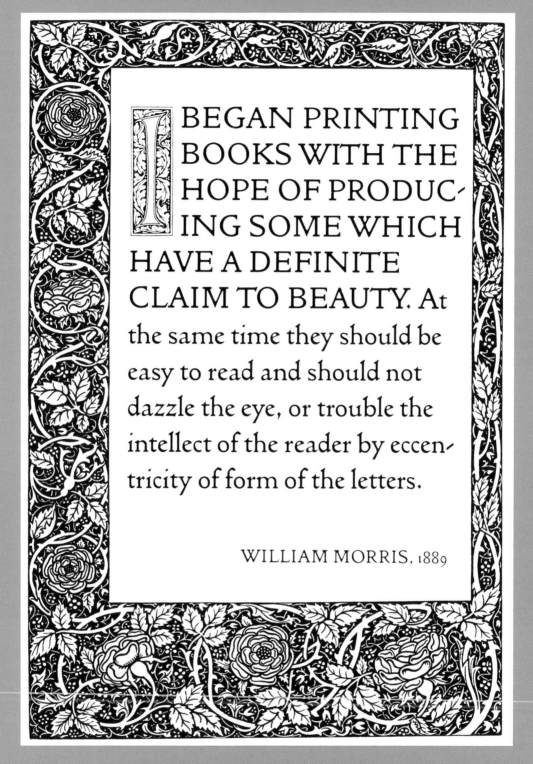

I BEGAN PRINTING BOOKS WITH THE HOPE OF PRODUC‑ING SOME WHICH HAVE A DEFINITE CLAIM TO BEAUTY. At the same time they should be easy to read and should not dazzle the eye, or trouble the intellect of the reader by eccen‑tricity of form of the letters.

WILLIAM MORRIS, 1889

Golden Type from 'ITC masterworks'.

How are these things interpreted nowadays by contemporary international letter designers with all the new digital input available to them? To what degree do cultural backgrounds, conventions and knowledge of the past still play a significant role? How are former views being reinterpreted and how relevant are they?

Actually, not that much has changed in the representation of the letter, but technology has made things easier. The process still begins with an idea, sometimes a hasty sketch to quickly record the idea and then, if it proves to be a good concept, the details are worked out. The next morning, the sketch from the day before often turns out not to be quite as innovative as the designer initially imagined.

What kind of character should letters have and what aspects of that character should their content convey? Is the client a newspaper, are we designing a 'fun and funky' letter using our own initiative or does a big city like Milan need a new style for its communications strategy?

What I find most striking is that letter designers, with their wonderful eye for detail, can create such great differences in the character of a letter. Erik van Blokland's Kosmik and Akira Kobayashi's Silvermoon are worlds apart. Or, compare Karlgeorg Hoefer's Sho with Hermann Zapf's Zapfino – the page naturally looks totally different. As reader or consumer, we perceive the message differently, too.

Clarendon's heyday was in the 1950s
and 1960s.
Two new cuts from D. Stempel A.G.:
Clarendon light and bold [above].
Monotype New Clarendon 617 [below].

'Monotype' New Clarendon 617   *6-72 point*

ABCDEFGHIJ

abcdefghij

KLMNOPQRST

klmnopqrst

UVWXYZ&ÆŒ

uvwxyzæœ

1234567890

The typographer's creation and the application of the graphic designer transport us to another world ruled by the dynamics of letterpress, the dynamism of digital technology and the impeccable prestidigitation of typographic wizards.

Handwritten faces and lead letterforms, the basis of typography.
New letters. There are always new letters that are different 'better, more beautiful'. For more than 500 years, the photosetting technique dictated the form, but, luckily, the computer has changed all that. These days, anything is possible digitally, and old lead and photoset letters are now being digitized. Is this a good or a bad thing? Regardless of the answer, it is unavoidable.

You cannot transform old lead letters at the drop of a hat. All digital fonts are programmed, whereas, in the lead era, all fonts were drawn and cast separately. Since 1990, new norms and aesthetic values have emerged. It seems that there is even more attention to detail, to handwork, to the master's eye. All the subtle differences in shape can be accommodated with ascender thicknesses, curves and serifs. Now, the designer has every opportunity to realize his dreams. The speed of adjusting individual fonts in the design process is optimal: thicker, thinner, italic, more open, all can be achieved in a flash. An extensive family of faces can be designed and produced in no time at all.

Recent aesthetic developments are probably more interesting than the technology, as reflected in the letters in this book. Sometimes the past

An original and interesting typeface, Peignot (1937) was designed by A.M. Cassandre (1901, Kharkov, the Ukraine–1968, Paris). Here, we see two pages of proofs, produced by Deberny et Peignot, Paris.

An original and interesting type face, "Peignot," designed by the famous French poster artist, A. M. Cassandre, and produced by Deberny et Peignot, Paris, has resulted in considerable discussion among typographic authorities. That the design is radical yet readable is indicated by the accompanying reproductions. "The Peignot type, intended for use in printing, is conceived as an engraved letter and not as a written letter," states the LIGHT

An original and interesting type face, "Peignot," designed by the famous French poster artist, A. M. Cassandre, and produced by Deberny et Peignot, Paris, has resulted in considerable discussion among typographic authorities. That the design is radical yet readable is indicated by the accompanying reproductions. "The Peignot type, intended for use in printing, is conceived as an engraved MEDIUM

An original and interesting type face, "Peignot," designed by the famous French poster artist, A. M. Cassandre, and produced by Deberny et Peignot, Paris, has resulted in considerable discussion among typographic authorities. That the design is radical yet readable is indicated by the accompanying reproductions. "The Peignot type, intended for use in printing, is BOLD

ALPHABET
MEDIUM 72 POINT

A A B b C c D d E e F f G g
H H I i J j K k L l M m N n
O o P p Q q R r S s T t U u
V v W w X x Y y Z z

1 2 3 4 5 6 7 8 9 0
1 2 3 4 5 6 7 8 9 0

comes back to life, as in Avenir and its beautiful, serious re-release by
the maestro himself, Adrian Frutiger. New requirements demand new letters.
It is a never-ending process that produces many fun types, such as
Erik van Blokland and Just van Rossum's Beowolf, and sometimes results
in completely new possibilities. Letters are being re-read and adapted,
changed or re-designed; that is the way it has always been. There are no
less than 400 different Bodonis, probably because people always think they
can improve or add something. New is better?!

I hope you will derive a great deal of pleasure from looking at and reading
Creative Type.

Cees W. de Jong, Laren

AntwortFax der Original BeowolfRandomDesigners! Idee: Erik van Blokland und Just van Rossum (1989) Schrift: Gestaltung Erik van Blokland (1988) Programm: IkarusM und dann von Hand in der PostScript code gehackt. Andere Schriften lassen sich erstmal nicht ändern, aber wir arbeiten dran. Die Schrift wird gekauft von vielen Leuten die interessiert sind an Typografie, und bereit sind das Abenteuer der RandomFonts an zu gehen. Die Fonts sind da um gegen die allgemeine Glattheit der Adobe u.a. Fonts ein Gegengewicht zu setzen. Nah, ein Zielgruppe gibt's eigentlich nicht- oder vielleicht Leute mit Macintosh Computers und Laserdrucker, die etwas von Typo wissen. Nutzen? RandomFonts sehen einfach gut aus, und machen Riesenspaß beim Farb-trennung weil jede Farbe anders wird. Das offizielle FontShop Zahl zur RandomFont verkauf ist 20. (das kann ja aber auch ziemlich zufällig sein) grüß Erik van Blokland+Just van Rossum, FontShop

The finishing touches for Beowolf were applied on the screen.

'Never do what anyone else has done before.
Always do things differently.'
Kurt Schwitters' guiding principle.

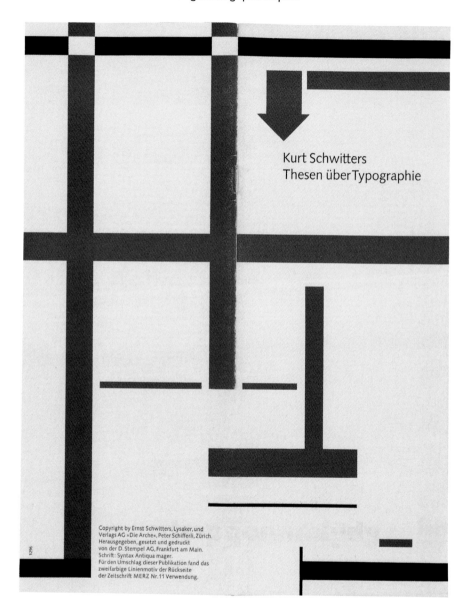

Kurt Schwitters
Thesen über Typographie

Copyright by Ernst Schwitters, Lysaker, und
Verlags AG »Die Arche«, Peter Schifferli, Zürich.
Herausgegeben, gesetzt und gedruckt
von der D. Stempel AG, Frankfurt am Main.
Schrift: Syntax Antiqua mager.
Für den Umschlag dieser Publikation fand das
zweifarbige Linienmotiv der Rückseite
der Zeitschrift MERZ Nr. 11 Verwendung.

Schwitters' book on typography was set
in Syntax in the 1960s. The front cover,
realized in two colours, was designed
by MERZ No.11.

Pages showing Stempel Syntax Antiqua,
1972 [opposite, top] and Stempel
Syntax Antiqua Extra Bold, Stempel AG,
1972 [opposite, bottom].

ABCDEF GHIJKLMNOPQ RSTUVWXYZ

Syntax Antiqua

extrafett

abcdef

ghijklmnopqrstu

vwxyzß

1234567890

D. Stempel AG 6 Frankfurt 70 Postfach 701160 Telefon (0611) 610391

Walter Schnackenberg (1880,
Lauterberg–1961, Wasserburg, Germany).
Kunstanstalt O. Consee, ca. 1918.

Waldemar Swierzy (1931, Krakow,
Poland), poster, 1959.

Anonymous, poster, Austria, 1954.

W. Roligkawnej, poster, Poland.

Waldemar Swierzy, poster, 1965.

Anonymous, poster, Germany, 1970.

In 1917, an exhibition of advertising art took place at the Stedelijk
Museum in Amsterdam, occasioning a lively debate between the artist
and designer R. N. Roland Holst (1868–1938) and the political cartoonist
Albert Hahn (1877–1918). Roland Holst held in contempt those
artists who, in his eyes, sold themselves for commercial purposes. He
maintained that the text for an advertisement could either clearly
present facts or else be a 'shout', and since truth did not have to be
exaggerated, shouts were little more than visual histrionics. Hahn,
though, took the more progressive stance and considered the shout quite
appropriate for the modern age. This dichotomy becomes clear when
one compares their posters from the same period. The letterforms of
Roland Holst display a quiet symmetry, while Hahn's have the energy
of a visual steam drill.

A few years later, the first and traditional approach was further
illustrated by the title of an essay, 'Printing Should Be Invisible', by the
typographic historian Beatrice Becker Warde (wife of American
typographer and type designer Fredric Warde), writing under the
pseudonym Paul Beaujon. According to her, typography should be
subordinate to the writer, and content, clarity and legibility should be
the principle objectives. The second approach, and subject of this essay,
is far different indeed. Here type has an autonomous function,
emphasizing the associative and plastic possibilities of letterforms.
Expressive solutions are achieved through the application of various
means, including contrasts of size, colour, structure, weight, form, texture
and direction, within the letterforms and in relation to the image; quite
often these contrasts are seen in combination.

As implied by the title, this is not intended as a chronological or
historical statement. Instead, it is a personal commentary on various
approaches to the expressive use of letters in graphic design over the past
century. For want of space, I have narrowed my focus to a few pivotal
figures whose designs stand out during this period of spirited innovation,
and broad categories were chosen to provide a rough framework to
accommodate work of wide diversity. However, even as examples are
placed in particular sections to illustrate various approaches (as design

This poster was designed by Jan Theodoor Toorop (1858, Java–1928, The Hague) in 1894 for the Delft Salad Oil factories. It was used for several years and made such a lasting impression that when the Dutch refer to 'Salad-Oil Style' they mean Art Nouveau.

36

Leonetto Cappiello (1875, Livorno,
Italy–1942, Nice, France), poster, 1901.

Thomas Theodor Heine (1867, Leipzig, Germany–1948, Stockholm, Sweden), poster, 1919.

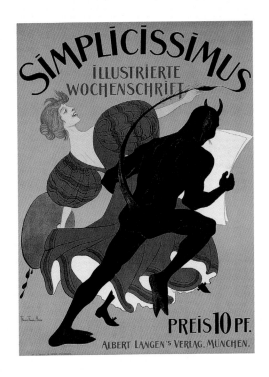

Jacob Jongert (1883–1942, the Netherlands), poster, c. 1920.

historians delight in doing), they will inevitably have other attributes that transcend any simplistic labels.

In addition to emphasizing contrast, designers also use letterforms as integrated elements within a composition. This is especially true with Art Nouveau, the extravagant fin-de-siècle style inspired by such sources as medieval manuscripts, natural forms and decorative arts from India, Syria, Egypt, Persia, Japan and the former Dutch East Indies. Lavish contours derived from flower stems and vines are common to this style. Jan Toorop's poster for Delft Salad Oil [see p. 35], printed in 1894, is a prime example of Art Nouveau, with its two goddess-like figures with spidery fingers preparing an extraordinary salad. However, the product being promoted is nearly lost in the torrent of interwoven lines. Twenty-three peanuts, framed by a vine in the upper-left corner, resemble a maze-like garden, and the standing goddess gazes at them, the NOF company logo and the product name with reverence. The text gracefully blends with the illustration, a common feature in Toorop's use of lettering.

To some extent a consequence of Art Nouveau and Cubism, Art Deco was the favourite international style during the late 1920s and early 1930s. However, unlike the luscious forms of Art Nouveau, Art Deco's forms are unemotional with a machine-like geometrical structure and, as with the Futurists, velocity and force are recurring themes. In Paris, the Art Deco designer A.M. Cassandre (1901–68), born Adolphe Jean-Marie Mouron in the Ukrainian city of Kharkov, adopted the ideas of such contemporary artists as Fernand Léger (1881–1955) and Le Corbusier (1887–1965) and applied them to poster design. As an indication of his respect for lettering, he designed Bifur in 1929 [see p. 57], the most popular Art Deco display face, and Peignot in 1937.

In Cassandre's 1924 poster for 'pi Volo Aperitif' the elements combine to form a single image as the lettering mirrors the shape of a wine glass and the silhouette of a bird. His 1927 poster for the North Star night train from Paris to Amsterdam also displays his ability to fuse lettering and image as the train rails merge with the lettering of 'Étoile du Nord' and much of the remaining information serves as a frame for the entire poster. Paul Colin (1892–1986), another French Art Deco artist, also binds text and image in his 1927 poster, 'André Renaud'.

Three posters by Swiss designers Niklaus Stoecklin (1896–1982), Herbert Leupin (1916–99) and Otto Baumberger (1889–1961) are notable in that the only letterforms are the product labels. In Stoecklin's 1941

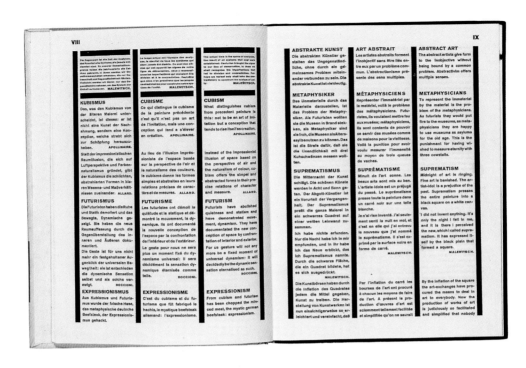

Pages VIII–IX and 18–19 of the book
Kunstismen 1914–24 by El Lissitzky and
Hans Arp, published in 1925 by Eugen
Rentsch Verlag in Erlenbach-Zurich,
Switzerland.

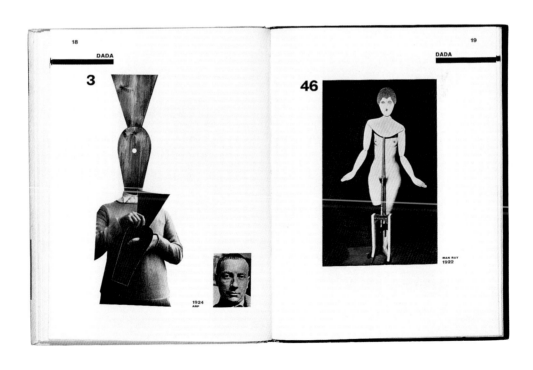

El Lissitzky's design of the front cover and
pages 34–35 and 56–57 of Vladimir
Maykovsky's book *Dlya Golosa/Zum Vorlesen*,
published in Berlin, 1923.

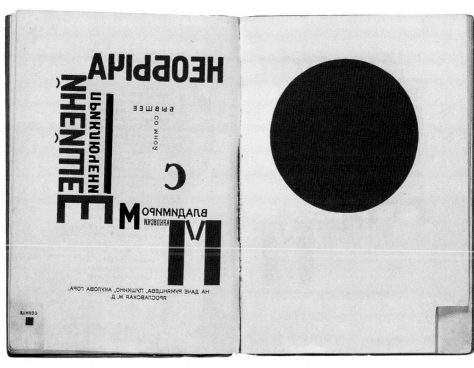

poster for Bi-ORO suntan lotion, the product's tube forms the entire message; in Leupin's striking 1949 poster for the Swiss newspaper, *Die Weltwoche,* the rolled paper is used as the top part of an exclamation mark with the paper's name boldly displayed; and in Baumberger's PKZ poster advertising winter overcoats, the only lettering is the small coat label.

For his 1910 Manoli cigarette poster [opposite], Lucian Bernhard's choice of type echoes his circular trademark for the company. In Hans Rudi Erdt's (1883–1918) 'Never Fail' poster the dot of the lowercase 'i' evolves into a row of buttons on the guard's coat, and Herbert Matter's (1907–84) lettering subtly accentuates the elongation of the sculpture in the poster for a Giacometti Exhibition in Basel (c. 1960).

Polish designers developed a unique visual identity during the 1950s and 1960s. In their designs, especially for posters, they used photography, illustration and handlettering, while freely employing symbolism, metaphors and shades of Surrealism. Among the more notable designers are Henryk Tomaszewski (b. 1914), Jan Lenica (b. 1928), Roman Cieslewicz (1930–96) and Waldemar Swierzy (b. 1931). Swierzy makes the painterly lettering an extension of the lipstick in his enchanting poster 'Ulilca Hanby' created in 1959 [see p. 31].

The German artist Hans Richter (1888–1976) presents his emotional hand-drawn lettering with the same ferocity as the images in his 1919 poster '3 Worte: Ungestorte Demobilmachung, Aufbauder Republik, Frieden' ('3 Words: Undisturbed Demobilization, Erect the Republic, Peace'). Boldly slashing through the photographic image with a diagonal line of brilliant red sans-serif type, the 'Less Noise' poster by Swiss designer Josef Müller-Brockmann (1914–96) generates a form of visual cacophony, the social issue that the poster is intended to be addressing.

Type becomes the building itself in the Jacobus Hooykaas (1903–69) poster for the 1930 opening of the new Bijenkorf department store in Rotterdam. In Alexander Schawinsky's (1904–79) 1934 Mussolini poster, three-dimensional letters serve as containers for images and additional text. Using an airbrush the Dutch designer Jan Lavies (b. 1902) skillfully constructs the letters 'Essolube', while letters framing an orgy assume the shape of the top of a bowler hat in Peter Max's (b. 1937) famous Toulouse-Lautrec poster.

An element of play maintains a ubiquitous presence in expressive typography. Designs by maverick Dutch artist Hendrik Nicolaas Werkman (1882–1945) are characterized by playfulness, serendipity and

Lucian Bernhard (1883, Stuttgart, Germany–1972, New York, USA), 1911. This design for cigarettes goes back to the simplest forms. Only Raymond Loewy would go on to be even more abstract in his work for Lucky Strike.

Waldemar Swierzy (1931, Krakow, Poland).

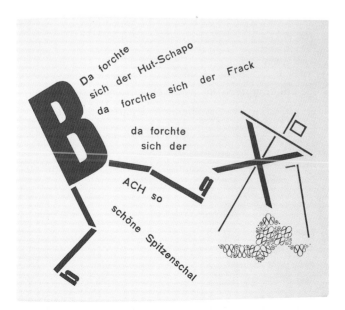

The brothers Georgi Stenberg (1900,
Russia–1933, USSR) and Vladimir
Augustovich Stenberg (1899, Moscow,
Russia–1982, USSR) designed this
promotional material for the French
film, *The Miracle of the Wolves*
(c. 1927).

Jan Tschichold (1902–74, Germany).
Photolithography and linocut for Kunst
im Druck GmbH, Munich, 1928.

NACHT DER LIEBE
MIT VILMA BANKY U. RONALD COLMAN

PHOEBUS
PALAST

ANFANG:
4⁰⁰ 6¹⁵ 8³⁰
SONNTAGS:
1⁴⁵ 4⁰⁰ 6¹⁵ 8³⁰

TSCHICHOLD

DRUCK: KUNST IM DRUCK GMBH MÜNCHEN

experimentation. Through using the basic letterpress, such subtleties as the oddities of wood grains, scratches on used pieces of type, disparate methods of inking and paper textures all contribute to his oeuvre. Despite the influence of Dada and Constructivism, Werkman always remained a phenomenon, a non-conformist and an outsider.

In September 1923, Werkman published the first of nine issues of *The Next Call*, an intermittently published magazine displaying experimental typography and Dada-inspired texts. The sixth issue was called 'Plattegrond van de Kunst en Omstreken' ('Map of Art and Environs') and was the first of two fold-out issues. The title originated from a casual remark by the painter Job Hansen when he saw Werkman at work on the composition: 'It looks like a map of art and its perimeters'. Werkman then added words and blocks forming pieces of land, lines indicating streets and rivers, and an arc of letters depicting the word *omstreken* (environs). Dated September 1925, the eighth issue of *The Next Call* has an implied association with industry, and the construction on the cover suggests a factory belching typographic smoke [opposite].

The playful typographic children's book *Die Scheuche* (*The Scarecrow*) appeared as one of Kurt Schwitters' Merz publications in 1925. Although the typography was by Theo van Doesburg (1883–1931), this was a joint effort with Schwitters (1887–1948) and Käte Steinitz with whom Schwitters had earlier collaborated on the children's books *De Hahnepeter* (*The Rooster*) and *Die Märchen von Paradies* (*Fairy Tales of Paradise*). Steinitz recalled Van Doesburg saying, 'Could we not create another picture book, one even more radical with only typographic elements?' Figures are created from elements of lowercase and uppercase lettering; for example, an uppercase 'B' functions as the body of an angry farmer, while each foot is represented by a lowercase 'b'.

The poster was an important propaganda tool during World War II, and the United States government conducted an energetic campaign to persuade Americans to enrol in the armed forces, purchase war bonds and work in industry. A notable example is the poster 'America's Answer: Production' by Jean Carlu (1900–89), the renowned French Art Deco designer stranded in the United States at the outbreak of the war. In this work, a sturdy gloved hand tightens a bolt with a wrench and, as a visual pun, the nut also serves as the first 'o' in the word 'Production'.

In the lively 1955 'Jazz' poster for Phillips Records by Dutch designer Cornelius van Velsen (b. 1921), the saxophone functions as a 'J' and an 'I' represents the torso and an arm and a leg of the performer.

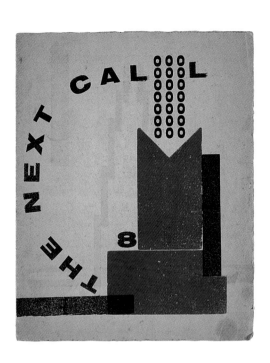

Hendrik Nicolaas Werkman (1882, Leens–1945, Bakkeveen, the Netherlands) designed and printed the front cover and inside pages of *The Next Call 8*, Groningen (the Netherlands), 1925.

Piet Zwart (1885, Zaandijk–1977, Leidschendam, the Netherlands) created the front cover and 4 pages of a calendar booklet with information on wire cables produced by the Netherlands Cable Works Ltd (NKF) in 1926.

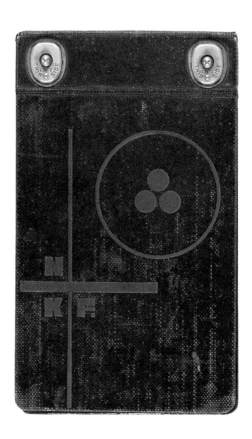

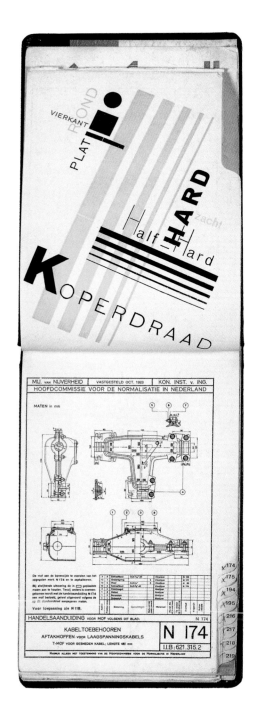

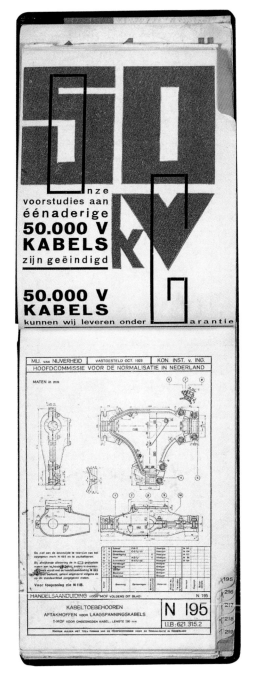

In Ghislain Escher's (b. 1945) poster to promote the Shafty Theater in 1974, the top point of the star also functions as the letter 'A'.

Willem J.H.B. Sandberg (1897–1984), director of the Stedelijk Museum in Amsterdam from 1945 to 1962, often made letters from torn paper, a technique later used by Yusaku Kamekura (1915–97) in Japan. Contrasting the rough edges with sans-serif type heightened the effect [opposite]. Roman Cieslewicz also created letters from ripped paper in his 1961 opera poster 'Persefoni'.

Type as texture was a popular device, especially during the so-called 'psychedelic' period in the 1960s as designers celebrated the anti-establishment sub-culture. In California, the most influential person working in this genre was Victor Moscoso (b. 1936), who achieved vibrant optical effects through colour and letterforms distorted almost to the point of illegibility. Moscoso was one of the few members of this group who had artistic training, having taken the colour course under Joseph Albers at Yale. Robert Wesley 'Wes' Wilson (b. 1937), another originator of this style, actually admitted that his colours were sometimes the result of experiments with LSD. Both Moscoso and Wilson regularly used a recycled version of Alfred Roller's (1864–1935) Vienna Secessionist alphabet.

The repetition of outline generates a textured surface in Lance Wyman's (b. 1937) lettering for the 1966 nineteenth Olympic Games logo. Mexican artistic traditions are also implied in the design of the five rings integrated with the number 66 and the word Mexico. Joining Olivetti as a designer in 1936, Italian Giovanni Pintori (1912–98) was art director from 1950 to 1968; as in his 1949 Olivetti poster, where the company's mission is implied through a carefully controlled layered texture of numbers, he often resorted to a cryptic, poetic style where the only reference to the client was its name.

The book designs of El Lissitzky (1890–1941), the most influential Russian constructivist, combined abstraction and functionalism with illustrations made from printing material. In his 1923 cover for Vladimir Mayakovsky's *Dlya Golosa/Zum Vorlesen* (*For the Voice*), the right angle created by vertical and horizontal lines of text is deftly counterbalanced by the circles and diagonal shapes [see p. 40].

Van Doesburg and others, including Bart Anthony van der Leck (1876–1958) and Piet Mondrian (1872–1944), founded De Stijl in 1917, the most significant Dutch iconoclastic artistic response to the carnage of World War I. A principal objective was to cleanse art of the past by eliminating subject matter, illusion, ornamentation and, above all,

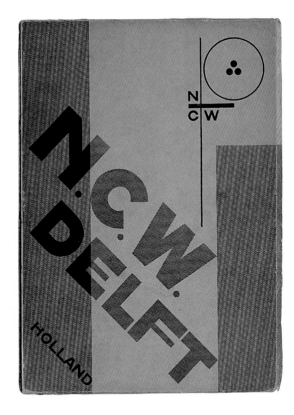

Piet Zwart's design for the front cover of the English edition of his catalogue for the Netherlands Cable Works Ltd (NKF).

Willem J.H.B. Sandberg (1897, Amersfoort–1984, Amsterdam, the Netherlands) produced the cover of the Stedelijk Museum's library catalogue in 1957 in Amsterdam.

A.M. Cassandre, (1901, Kharkov, the Ukraine–1968, Paris, France) produced this enamel sign in 1929, the Netherlands.

In 1928, the Olympics were to be held in Amsterdam and this poster, by Cassandre, promoted rail transportation there.

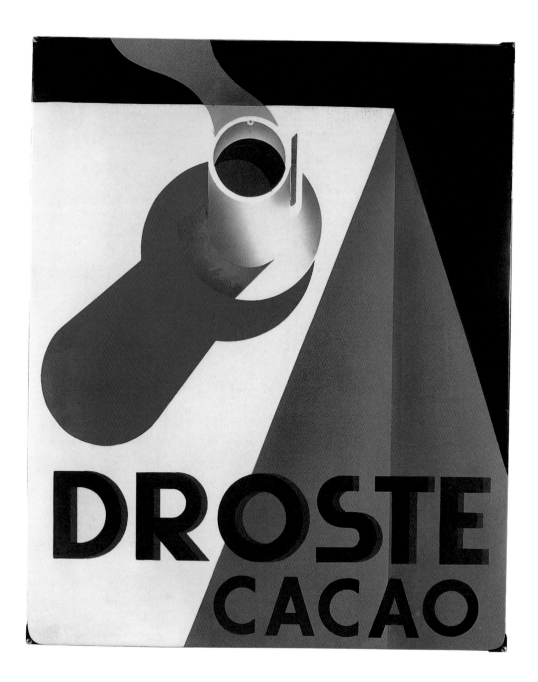

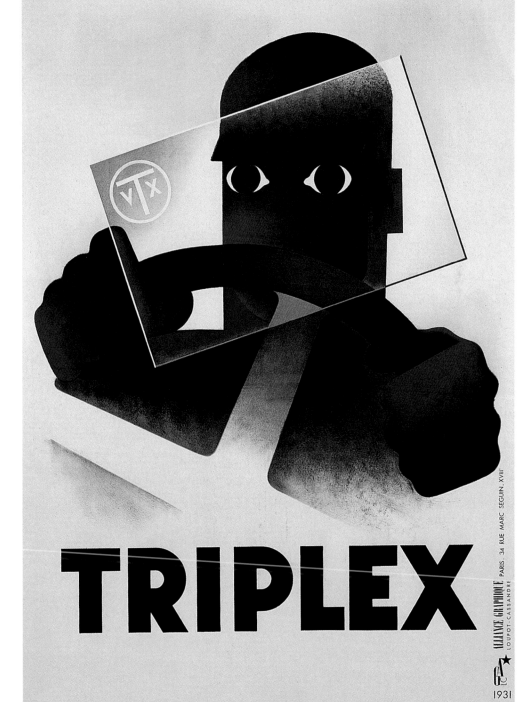

subjectivity. The first volume of their official journal, *De Stijl*, was published in October 1917, with the first three volumes designed by Vilmos Huszar (1884–1960). At the end of 1920, Van Doesburg and Mondrian redesigned the overall format of *De Stijl* to reflect Van Doesburg's interest in El Lissitzky's typographic structure.

Van der Leck abstracted his subjects into compositions of lines, geometric forms and related fragmented stencil-like letters as seen in the 1919 Delft Salad Oil poster design. This was the final of twelve versions rejected by the board of directors, largely because the poster's subject, a salad oil bottle, could hardly be detected.

Piet Zwart (1885–1977) and Paul Schuitema (1897–1973) were leading Dutch constructivists. Trained as an architect, Zwart began working in graphic design at the age of thirty-six, and, although influenced by De Stijl, he rejected its reliance on horizontals and verticals. In 1938, Zwart referred to his method as functional typography. Like the Russian constructivists, he saw his task as creating 'the typographical look of our time, free in so far as it is possible from tradition; to activate typographic forms to find clear and ordered visual ways of expression, to define the shape of new typographic problems, methods and techniques and to discard the guild mentality.'

Zwart called himself a 'typotekt', a combination of the words typographer and architect, and saw the graphic designer's essential mission as one of constructing with typographic material and other visual elements, as an architect would design a building. Especially in the cover design, El Lissitzky's influence is highly evident in Zwart's 1926 calendar booklet providing information on wire cables manufactured by the Netherlands Cable Works Ltd [see pp 48–49].

Schuitema believed that 'every item, every letter, every picture, every sound, every colour should have its function.' For the cover for the January 1926 issue of the magazine *De Fakkel*, he combined letters with rectangular shapes to build an architectural structure.

As evidenced by the magazine *Wendingen* launched by Dutch architect Hendricus Theodorus Wijdeveld (1885–1987) in 1918, architecture and graphic design can be closely related fields. Ostensibly *Wendingen* was a publication devoted mainly to architecture, construction and ornamentation, but during its thirteen-year life, it represented all sectors of the visual arts. The 33-x-33cm pages were printed on one side, folded and sewn with raffia, in the Japanese block book style. Each issue was devoted to a single subject with a place for advertisements in the back. In addition to constructing ornaments from printing materials,

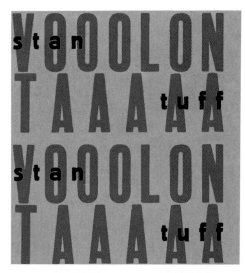

Filippo Achille Emilio Marinetti (1879, Alexandria, Egypt–1944, Bellagio, Italy). Four pages from his futurist book, *Parole in Liberta*, printed on metal, 1932.

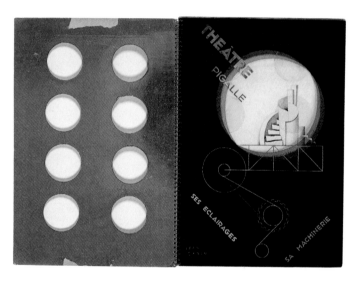

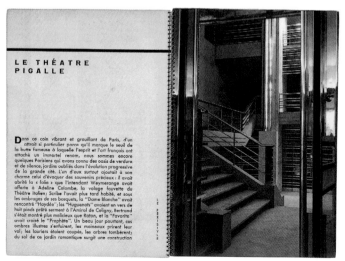

LE THÉATRE
PIGALLE

Dans ce coin vibrant et grouillant de Paris, d'un
attrait si particulier parce qu'il marque le seuil de
la butte fameuse à laquelle l'esprit et l'art français ont
attaché un immortel renom, nous sommes encore
quelques Parisiens qui avons connu des oasis de verdure
et de silence, jardins oubliés dans l'évolution progressive
de la grande cité. L'un d'eux surtout ajoutait à son
charme celui d'évoquer des souvenirs précieux : il avait
abrité la « folie » que l'intendant Weymerange avait
offerte à Adeline Colombe, la volage fauvette du
Théâtre Italien; Scribe l'avait plus tard habité, et sous
les ombrages de ses bosquets, la "Dame Blanche" avait
rencontré "Haydée"; les "Huguenots" avaient en vers de
huit pieds prêté serment à l'Amiral de Coligny, Bertrand
s'était montré plus malicieux que Raton, et la "Favorite"
avait croisé le "Prophète". Un beau jour pourtant, ces
ombres illustres s'enfuirent, les moineaux prirent leur
vol; les lauriers étaient coupés, les arbres tombèrent;
du sol de ce jardin romantique surgit une construction

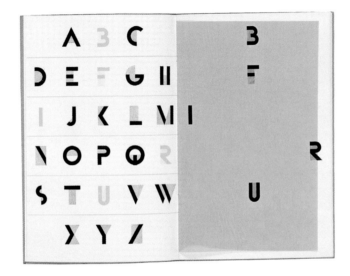

Jean George Leon Carlu (1900, Bonnières-sur-Seine, France–1997, Paris) created this 1929 cover, title spread and pages 6–7 of a promotional booklet for the Theatre Pigalle.

A.M. Cassandre designed the front cover and pages 4–5 of a promotional booklet for Bifur, a letter designed by Cassandre and printed by Deberny et Peignot, Paris, 1929.

Wijdeveld also created actual letters from right-angular elements, like a mason working with bricks.

The architect W.M. Dudok (1884–1974) produced two covers for *Wendingen*. Letterforms in his exceptional design for the eighth issue in 1924 are constructed from typesetting material and convey his own architectural style. Vilmos Huszar's typography for a 1929 *Wendingen* cover reflects the issue's theme: the political murals of Mexican painter Diego Rivera (1886–1957). The complementary colours red and green are those of the Mexican national flag, and patterns built up from geometric letters imply the friezes on Aztec architecture. This is the only instance that anyone connected with De Stijl contributed a *Wendingen* cover design, and, although Huszar had ended his association with De Stijl eight years earlier, the letters on the cover strongly resemble Van Doesburg's ponderous 1919 alphabet design.

Issues 3 to 9 of *Wendingen*, in 1925, were devoted to Frank Lloyd Wright (1867–1959), and the same design by Wijdeveld is used for all seven issues. Another notable Wijdeveld design is his 1929 poster for the Internationale Economisch-Historische Tentoonstelling (International Economics and History Exhibition), a typographic reflection of the brick architecture of the Amsterdam school.

Welcoming the modern age, the Italian futurists rejected old concepts of harmony and produced poems reflecting the noise and speed of the modern world. Futurism began when the Italian poet Filippo Marinetti (1879–1944) published his *Manifesto of Futurism* on 20 February 1909. On his cover and pages for the 1932 book *Parole in Liberta*, the visual poems clatter like the metal sheets on which they are printed [see p. 55].

Through stretching and bending the letters and contrasting receding type with advancing arrows, type is used to express movement and depth in Max Huber's (1919–92) poster 'Gran premio dell'Autodromo' for an automobile race in 1948. A native of Switzerland, Huber studied at the Bauhaus and the Zurich School of Arts and Crafts. He then worked as a designer in Milan, before and after World War II, where he produced phenomenal designs using pure colours and transparent layered inks. Expressing both perspective and speed, type becomes the road in Herbert Leupin's 1957 poster for the Renault Dauphine; while in his 1963 poster 'Wilhelm Tell', Swiss designer Armin Hofmann (b. 1920) typographically stresses the direction and velocity of the arrow as the letters of Tell's name rapidly diminish in size when approaching the apple target.

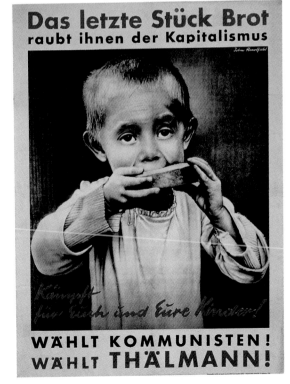

Valentina Nikiforovna Kulagina (Russia, 1902–87), poster, 1930.

John Heartfield (pseudonym for Helmut Herzfeld, 1892, Berlin, Germany–1968, East Berlin) designed this election poster in 1932. The photolithography is by S. Maltz, Berlin.

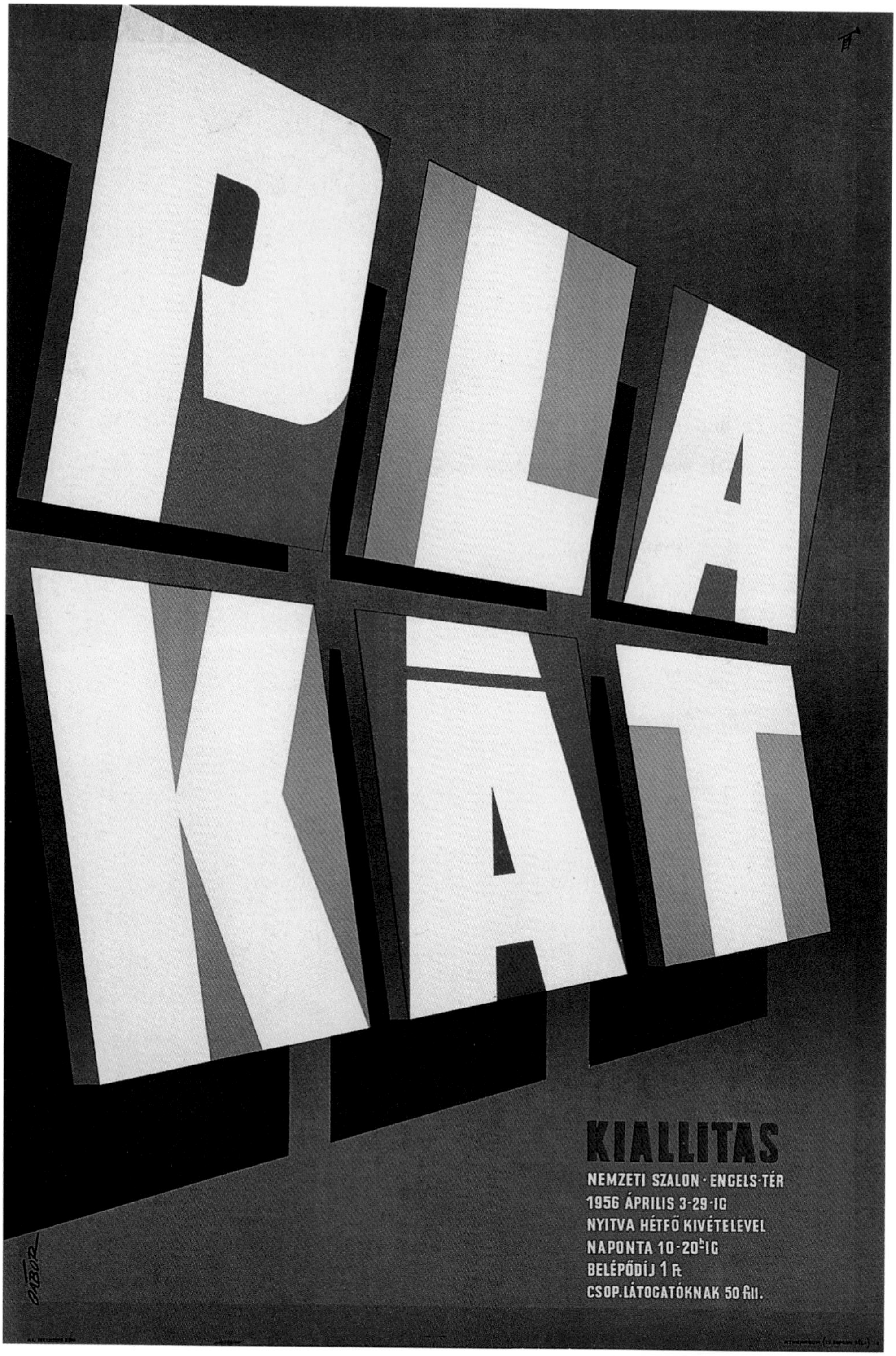

PILAKÁT

KIALLITAS
NEMZETI SZALON · ENGELS·TÉR
1956 ÁPRILIS 3·29·IG
NYITVA HÉTFŐ KIVÉTELEVEL
NAPONTA 10·20°IG
BELÉPŐDÍJ 1 Ft
CSOP.LÁTOGATÓKNAK 50 fill.

Gabor, poster, 1956, Athenaeum,
Poland.

Satomi, Munetsugu (1900–95, Japan),
1934, Côte d'Azur, PLM, Satomi Le
Novateur, Paris, France.

Today, designers, such as David Carson (b. 1956), push letterforms beyond all previously known limits. Rudy VanderLans (b. 1955) and his wife Zuzana Licko (b. 1961) continue to question all graphic design traditions, and the magazine *Emigre* is a forum for exploring expressive typography using computer technology. Dutch designer Gerard Hadders (b. 1954), originally part of the Rotterdam design group Hard Werken, represents another of many reactions to Formalism and Modernism. Like Dutch designer Max Kisman (b. 1953), Hadders rejects all previous styles with amazing results. For them and many of their generation, such as the exceptional and highly imitated British designer Neville Brody (b. 1957), conventional typographic canons are suspended until further notice.

Alston W. Purvis

Anonymous, 1962, Mokép film, Hungary.

Anonymous, c. 1970, United Kingdom.

64

Max Kisman (1953, Doetinchem, the Netherlands) designed this poster for a music festival in Amsterdam's Paradiso club, 1986.

Rudy VanderLans and Zuzana Licko's magazine *Emigre*, 1993.

From Rudolf Koch via David Carson into the New Millennium: Typography in the 20th Century

Rudolf Koch (1876–1934, Germany),
poster, 1919.

Jan Tschichold (1902–74, Germany),
cover for the magazine *Typographische
Mitteilungen*, 1925.

zeitschrift des bildungsverbandes der deutschen buchdrucker leipzig ● oktoberheft 1925

typographische mitteilungen

sonderheft

elementare typographie

natan altman
otto baumberger
herbert bayer
max burchartz
el lissitzky
ladislaus moholy-nagy
molnár f. farkas
johannes molzahn
kurt schwitters
mart stam
ivan tschichold

Alexander

Tairoff

DAS

ENTFESSELTE

THEATER

El Lissitzky (1890–1941, Russia), book
cover, 1927.

Anton Stankowski (1906–98, Germany),
poster, 1932.

History is, by necessity, a condensation of events. In a similar vein, the description of the history of typography in the twentieth century is an attempt to distinguish between the main flow and the tributaries of the past and to pinpoint major areas of development to ensure the description is comprehensive today.

The twentieth century was shaken by drastic changes and driven by idealism. As has always been the case through history, different views and styles fought for supremacy, while the burden of tradition still weighed heavily. In addition to aesthetic conflicts, dramatic technical changes also came about, which in themselves would have been enough to justify and to explain the innovations in design.

After the reformation movement of William Morris and later Peter Behrens, which was extremely significant for typography, developments in the late 1910s and early 1920s were divided between the subjective-expressive and functional elementary schools of thought.

The expressive position is often reflected in the work of Rudolf Koch [see p. 66], who sought the path of innovation by returning to individualism and pre-industrialization. On the other hand, functional typography, based on a social responsibility, was developed primarily by designers in the Netherlands, Hungary, the Soviet Union and Germany. It was a counter movement and a new beginning. Up against the static middle-of-the-road mentality venerating the craftsmanship of the common man and after the dead-end reactionary ideas that arose during World War I, there was a desire to develop a better social, cultural and future-oriented form of typography.

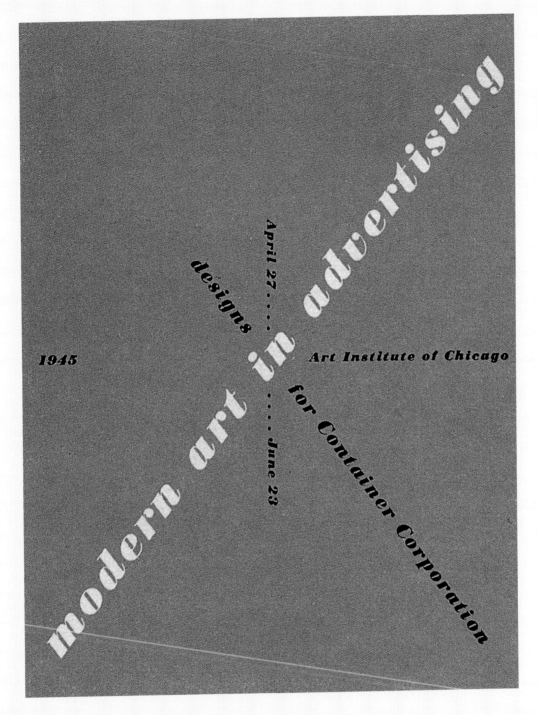

modern art in advertising

designs

April 27 . . . . . . June 23

1945

Art Institute of Chicago

for Container Corporation

Herbert Bayer (1900–85, Austria),
catalogue, 1945.

Achieved through reduction in ornaments and pragmatism in the choice of typographic elements, the major characteristics of the New Typography were sans-serif faces, lowercase lettering and asymmetrical spacing. As early as 1925, the first summary of the objectives and work of the Avant-garde was published as an appendix to the magazine *Typografische Mitteilungen*. Jan Tschichold, who had first worked for a brief period in the style of elementary typography, brought together such major designers as Herbert Bayer, Max Burchartz, El Lissitzky, László Moholy-Nagy and Kurt Schwitters.

Reflecting events in the political arena, however, progressive forces were resisted, overcome and suppressed in art and typography, too. Many typographers, therefore, had to change their style or emigrate. In Germany, archaic design rules were reintroduced and enforced. In Switzerland, the work of the young Anton Stankowski, who, after studying in Essen, worked as a graphic designer in Zurich from 1929 to 1937, earned a great deal of respect for the New Typography. It is thanks to him that New Typography evolved in Switzerland during the oppression in Germany and the rest of Europe and went on to gain fame in the 1940s and 1950s under the name *Schweitszer Typografie* (Swiss Style or International Typographic Style). The first generation included Max Bill, Richard P. Lohse, Max Huber and Emil Ruder.

In addition to the Swiss designers, Austrian-born Herbert Bayer, former leader of the Bauhaus typographic studio, worked with great success in the United States in the spirit of New Typography. The link between the strict dogmatism of the sans-serif face and the forms of the expanded American advertisements led to yet another interesting design form. Although Jan Tschichold, a pioneer and a propagandist of Modernism, was reconsidering the traditional values in his work in the 1940s, elementary typography had become the dominant, inescapable international style. Aside from the kitsch designs that lacked any form of progressive design

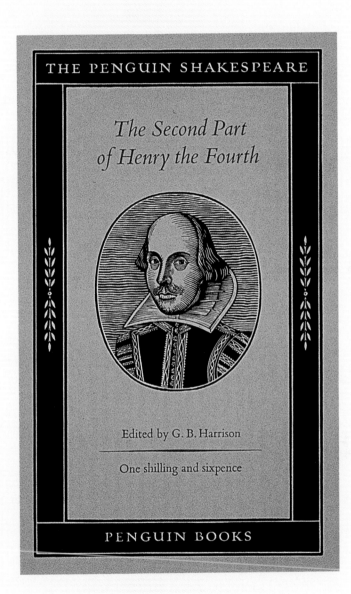

THE PENGUIN SHAKESPEARE

*The Second Part
of Henry the Fourth*

Edited by G. B. Harrison

One shilling and sixpence

PENGUIN BOOKS

Jan Tschichold (1902–74, Germany),
book cover, 1949.

quality and were – and still are – so strongly represented in mass communications, the work of Josef Müller-Brockmann and Mary Vieira in Switzerland, Isolde Baumgart and the *Novum-Gruppe* in the Federal Republic of Germany and Gene Federico and Herb Lubalin in the USA demonstrates the liveliness and creativity in the development of the New Typography: culture is only culture when it is progressive!

During the high point of brush and palette typesetting, a design academy was set up in Ulm, Germany in 1953 with the intention of breathing new life into the legacy of the Bauhaus, which had closed its doors in 1933. In view of the crazy consumer culture abounding in the Federal Republic, and with all the consequences that entailed, the state withdrew its financial support in 1968, forcing the closure of the school, which had been experiencing problems with the government from the beginning. Throughout its brief period of existence, the academy sought to simultaneously express ethics and aestheticism in design, leading to a great number of major developments in product design and work in visual communication that was for a long time the model for catchy typography, such as the Braun and Lufthansa corporate identities. In the early 1960s, deviations from the strict typographic rules of the Swiss Style were seen everywhere. The decline of elementary typography was chiefly due to the fact that commercial nitwits adopted these forms as ready-made concepts, and, once so intent on improving content, typographic communication lapsed into bureaucratic functionality. As so often happens, there was an interesting parallel with the simultaneous problem of style in architecture.

Another contributing factor to the loss of strict Grotesque typography was the immense quantity of undogmatic, innovative work coming from the USA, where a highly successful pictorial development in the use of letters and text combined with photographic representation was under way. Increasingly, graphic design became less a question of designing a

Max Huber (1919–92, Switzerland),
poster, 1948.

few pieces of printed material and more a matter of designing total concepts and series for international commercial communication.

One of the most striking examples is the series of advertisements for VW, which were distributed all over the world with hundreds of different texts, but always in an unmistakable design structure and in the Futura face.

From the mid-1960s, type became one of the most important ways to elaborate on a concept to arrive at a distinctive total presentation. One of the first fonts to be produced as a family in more than twenty cuts was Adrian Frutiger's Univers, which was more suitable for this purpose than other font families with their fewer, less coordinated cuts.

Concurrently, a drastic change in setting technology was taking place. For four hundred years, the lead setting system and its associated horizontal text liaison had limited the options; with the arrival of photosetting this changed to virtually unrestricted freedom of movement within the plane. What had only been achievable after a great deal of dedication and hard work in many Avant-gardist designs became easy to do and, therefore, common property. There was rapid access to the most diverse typefaces and the most extraordinary cuts. Modification enabled even better visualization of the content and word, and text and images could be set closer together. For a short time, the Letraset technique was one of the new creative options in typography. At this time, a group of designers were also interested in discipline in design, and the most interesting magazine on this subject was *Twen*, published between 1959 and 1970 and designed by Willy Fleckhaus.

A large part of the success of the German railway advertisements of that time was due to the use of the virtually neglected Gill extra-bold, which was seldom in stock for lead setting and matched the content of the adverts like no other face. Unfortunately, the possibility of cheap, fast, exotic faces also led to a lot of technical and aesthetic errors and, for a

Mary Vieira (1927, Brazil), poster,
Kunstgewerbe Museum, Zurich, 1954.

while, typography looked like a bad Wild West film. However, because of its technical refinement and rapid spread, photosetting allowed an unprecedented level of quality in typesetting and added sophistication to the design.

In the late 1960s, the belief in progress in the Western world led to a crisis in the interpretation of values. This was felt in the field of typography, where, for example, as an alternative to the omnipresent cool Helvetica, illustrative faces again emerged in solutions for communication assignments. This had nothing to do with a reactionary development in type; it was prompted more by esprit and spontaneity. Nevertheless, this aesthetic escape attempt was also rapidly integrated into official typography.

The typographic 1970s brought only a few great personalities and a number of extremely dull ones, but there were many mainstream designs, widely distributed in large quantities. It was the heyday of the renowned record-sleeve designs by the English studio Hypgnosis and the fantastic culture posters designed in photomontage by Holger Matthies, Frieder Grindler and the graphic-design partnership Rambow/Lienemeyer/van de Sand. In the advertising and promotion world, a number of classics with intelligence and charm emerged; conceptual designs free from dogmatic restrictions. The various departments of the GGK advertising agency produced a constant stream of creative work.

One of the greatest examples of functional design was Otl Aicher's corporate design for the 1972 Olympic Games in Munich [see p. 83], which gained great international recognition and proved, among other things, that Grotesque typography (in this case, Univers) was not bad, rather it was the creative solution that counted. There are no bad faces, only bad applications. Willy Fleckhaus' careful choice of font for the book sleeves for the publishing firm Suhrkamp Verlag and the jackets Heinz Edelmann designed for Klett-Cotta Verlag instilled new life into literary

Josef Müller-Brockmann (1914–96,
Switzerland), poster, 1960.

works for the young generation. Herb Lubalin's new Grotesque face, Avant Garde, was both vilified and venerated, owing its popularity largely to the design of the magazine *UPPER & lowercase*, first published in 1973 by the International Typeface Corporation in New York.

In addition to all these striking events, and for what was to be the last time in a long while, a philosophical and experimental design initiative formed the basis for further advances in international typography. A great deal of what Wolfgang Weingart developed with such diligence and creativity at the Kunstgewerbeschule in Basel in the 1970s looked strange and failed to be understood at the time, but it was to serve as a model for the typography of the 1980s. His international students spread the results of his training to the UK and the USA, where they were lifted from their scientific context into commercial design assignments and returned to Continental Europe under the New Wave label. A kind of cosmic, fleeting style emerged, highly distinctive and combining text and image. April Greiman and Michael Vanderbyl were amongst the young stars of these American West Coast designers.

While these innovations were under way in the West, typography in Japan was undergoing revolutionary changes that extended its influence to Europe and the USA from the end of the 1970s. The Japanese produced daring image and text collages and realized three-dimensional typographic structures using computers. Through such techniques, designers like Ikko Tanaka and Takenobu Igarashi gained worldwide recognition.

From the early 1980s, young people's interest in typography increased dramatically and unexpectedly. The unparalleled possibilities of 'playing' with computers generated new typographic concepts for such magazines in Europe and the USA as *Wet*, *Fetish* and *I.D.* It was at this time that one of the young, bright superstars of contemporary typography, Neville Brody [see p. 89], appeared, gaining fame primarily for his design of the magazine *The Face*.

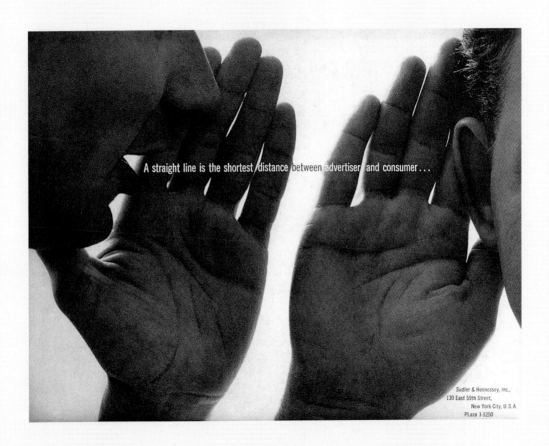

Herb Lubalin (1918–81, USA),
poster, 1956.

Some of the most extraordinary typographic results were achieved in the Netherlands: Wim Crouwel and his studio Total Design, which for some time previously had been synonymous with quality and innovation, succeeded in expressing the changing awareness of design in state assignments; and, with their Typo-Foto-Imagination technique, Studio Dumbar joined the ranks of the great modern Dutch traditionalists, within which two major pioneers of the New Typography, Piet Zwart and Paul Schuitema, were already working with great success. The style was dominated by collages, quotations, sly references and often typography bordering on illegibility (the reality was, however, that nothing was actually illegible).

More modest and without overnight success, another significant Willy Fleckhaus design, the *Frankfurter Allgemenie Magazin*, first saw the light of day in 1980 and went on to greatly influence the design world. As well as the classic and revolutionary typographic concepts, new functional concepts were also appearing. Siegfried Odermatt, one of the most creative designers in Switzerland in the 1960s, and his partner Rosmarie Tissi created new images without the help of advanced technology [see p. 88]. Otl Aicher developed an exciting elementary style for book typography. In Berlin, Ott + Stein's no-nonsense style and personal touch gave a new look to the cultural poster. The 8vo group in London brought new quality to the communication on typography with their magazine *Octavo*; on one hand, it was a militant pamphlet and a research platform and, on the other, a successful combination of form and content.

Like photosetting before it, the DTP technique, which meant a further major change in design, had got over its teething troubles. Although this rapidly accepted and widely spread process heralded a form of democratization within typography, it also posed the risk of design conformity, despite – or perhaps even because of – the excellent design programs. But, there have always been good and poor designers.

München ⬤⬤⬤⬤⬤ 1972

Otl Aicher (1922–91, Germany),
poster, 1972.

Page 85:
Heinz Edelmann (1942, Germany),
book cover, 1979.

A major new DTP technique was the creation of exciting running text structures, text forms that do not remain stuck in reader-unfriendly, dull grey monotony but tailor structure to content, thus making the text more readable. Text-image combinations also incorporated radically new elements clearly distinguishable from the simple designs of the 1960s. The typography of the 1990s was coloured by the infinite possibilities of electronic media. With the seemingly boundless possibilities of the new design programs, designers seeking uninhibited and commercially informative solutions achieved surprising forms in response to the communication challenges of the new era. For example, the English group Why Not Associates, with their innovative design philosophy, realized work that left an indelible print on the young visual spirit of the time.

Once again, the Netherlands produced undogmatic concepts, especially in the area of communication: Gerard Hadders astonished with his wackily dynamic designs for cultural institutions and Irma Boom produced exciting, versatile but apt book projects, which were seen as a manifestation and an acceptance of the design risks within visual communication.

In the USA, another typographic superstar was discovered; David Carson's work and ways of thinking served as an example for the new design generation [see p. 91]. His work was so well known and accepted that even the big multinationals took up his aesthetic proposals and used them in their communications.

Ed Fella [see p. 90] was exceptional and inaccessible; as a tried and trusted advertising man his design contributions were innovative, experimental combinations of the various alphabetic means of expression. In spite of any requirements, the scriptural, expressive, illustrative and typographic elements of Fella's designs fused and even elevated the concepts of 'free' and 'applied' design. He created unique, inventive and artistic designs within the typographic and communication world.

Die Wachstumsdebatte

E. J. Mishan

Wachstum zwischen
Wirtschaft und Ökologie
– Klett-Cotta –

Warum ein streng wissen-
schaftlicher Ansatz nichts taugt.
Ein alternativer Ansatz.
Was bei der Wachstumsdebatte unter
den Tisch fällt.
Die Hoffnungen verblassen.
Woraus das gute Leben besteht.
Technologie und Freiheit.

Aside from all the excessive forms and individual expressions that occupied such an important position throughout the twentieth century, cool, functional design ideas once more became popular in the 1990s in the form of previous trends or in the development of existing concepts. Barbara and Gerd Baumann rose to international fame for the substantial quantity of work they produced that, although without expressive individualistic form, exhibited an unmistakable new typographic design approach.

The passage of time blurs past contradictions in typography. The gigantic and fascinating range of old and new faces eliminates the previously important question of 'Antiqua or Grotesque'. These days, Helvetica, which had been written off in the 1970s, is again in common usage among the creative young generation.

The new variety in typography bodes well: more than ever and despite the new media, this ancient craft is consciously acknowledged, applied and understood. The current broad interest in the history of typography indicates that, in the future, we can expect more well-founded but unexpected new developments and ideas to come to the fore, leaving no room for nostalgic typographic melancholy.

Friedrich Friedl, 2005

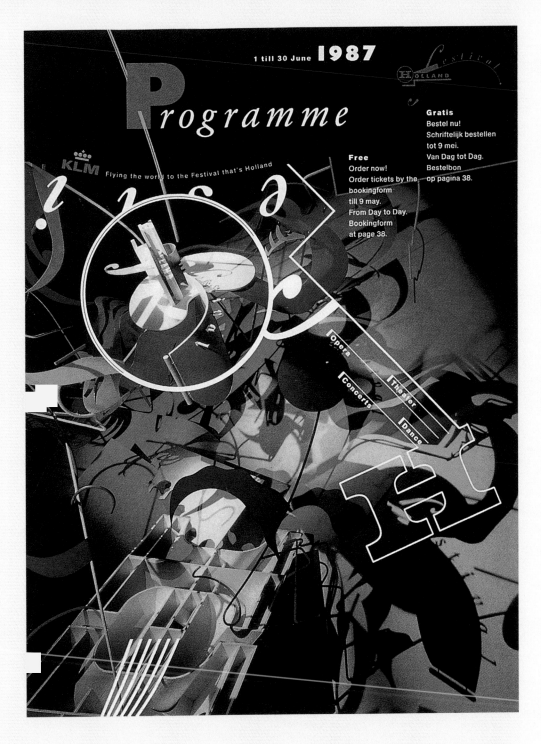

Gert Dumbar (1940, the Netherlands),
cover, 1987.

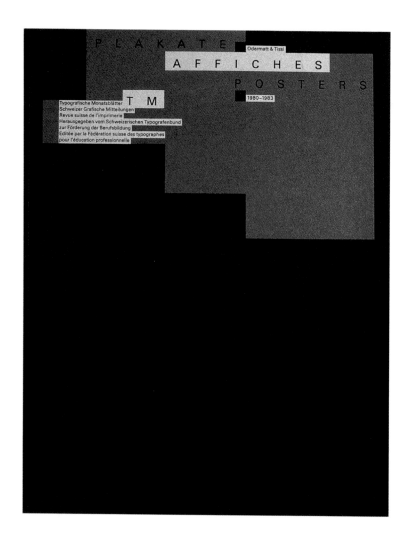

Siegfried Odermatt and Rosmarie Tissi
(Germany), magazine cover, 1979.

Neville Brody (1957, UK), poster, 1988.

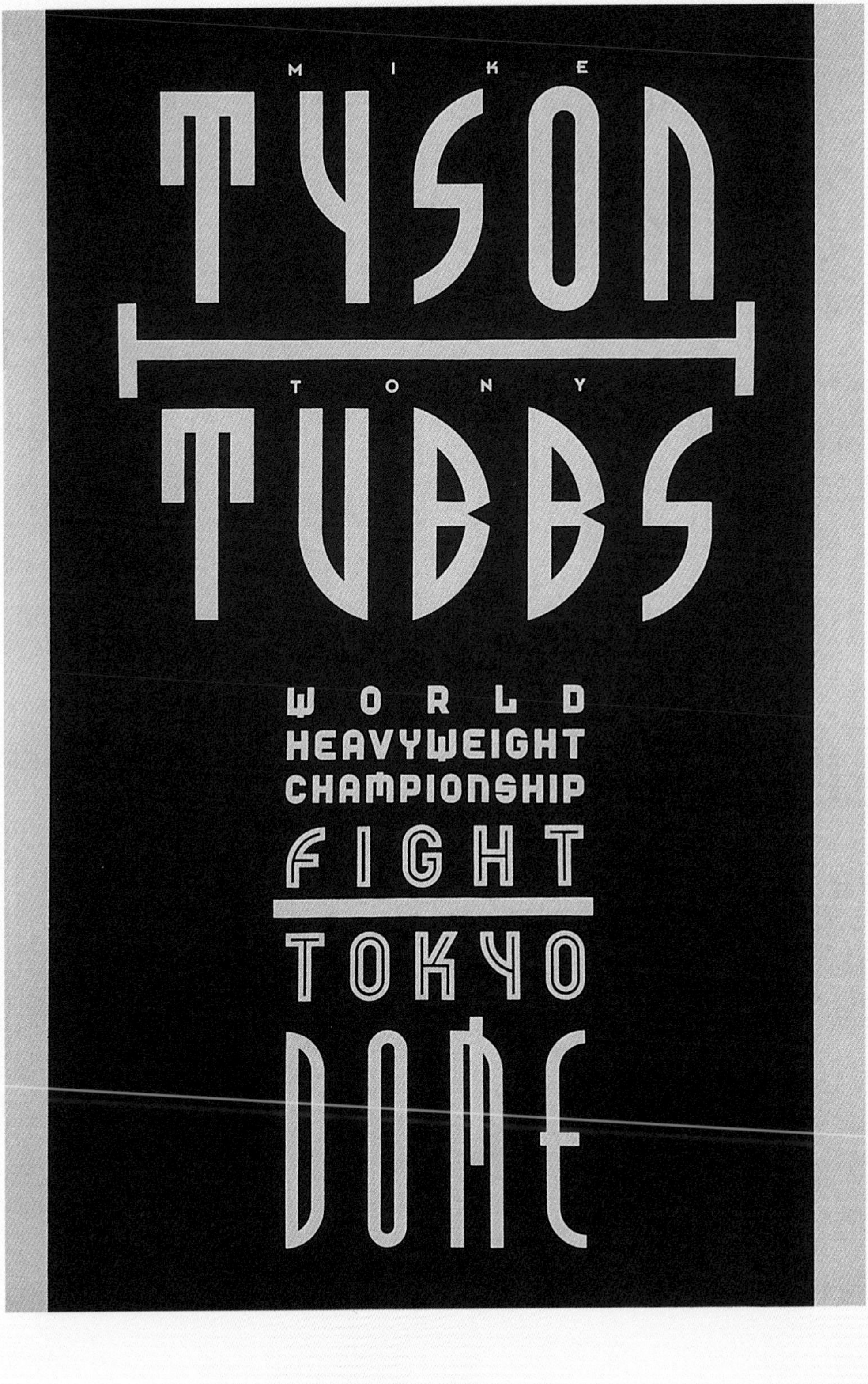

MIKE

TYSON

TONY

TUBBS

WORLD
HEAVYWEIGHT
CHAMPIONSHIP

FIGHT

TOKYO

DOME

Ed Fella (1938, USA), poster, 1995.

David Carson (1956, UK), book
cover, 1995.

THE END OF PRINT:

MUTAD

THE GRAPHIC DESIGN OF DAVID CARSON

BY LEWIS BLACKWELL & DAVID CARSON
INTRODUCTION BY DAVID BYRNE

ITC Franklin, 2004
David Berlow

Demos, 2004
Gerard Unger

Zapfino, 2003
Hermann Zapf

Kosmik, 2002
Erik van Blokland

Sabon Next, 2002
Jean François Porchez

Le Monde, 1997
Jean François Porchez

Linotype Syntax, 2000
Hans Eduard Meier

Aroma, 1999
Tim Ahrens

Gianotten, 1999
Antonio Pace

Markin, 1999
Alfred Tilp

Scarborough, 1998
Akira Kobayashi

Silvermoon, 1998
Akira Kobayashi

Atomatic, 1997
Johannes Plass

Finnegan, 1997
Jürgen Weltin

Spitz, 1997
Oliver Brentzel

Carumba, 1996
Jill Bell

Filosofia, 1996
Zuzana Licko

Tagliatelle, 1996
Alessio Leonardi

LinoLetter, 1992
Linotype

Linotype Didot, 1991
Linotype

Veto, 1994
Marco Ganz

Sho, 1992
Karlgeorg Hoefer

PMN Caecilia, 1990
Peter Matthias Noordzij

Officina, 1990
Erik Spiekermann

Industria, 1989
Neville Brody

Avenir, 1988
Adrian Frutiger

Frutiger Next, 2001
Adrian Frutiger

Stone, 1987
Sumner Stone

Lucida Sans, 1985
Kris Holmes/Charles Bigelow

Optima nova, 2002
Hermann Zapf

ITC Franklin – David Berlow – 2004

Franklin Gothic was created at the turn of the 20th century by Morris Fuller Benton.

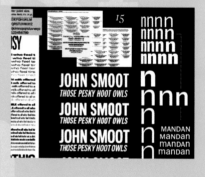

International Typeface Corporation and The Font Bureau Inc. worked on a multiphase project to update and enlarge the ITC Franklin Gothic typeface family. The expanded product was re-branded as the ITC Franklin family in 2005.

'Although an important mainstay in the ITC library for almost 25 years, the typeface is deserving of attention to bring it up-to-date and beyond,' said Allan Haley, director of words and letters at ITC. 'We turned to Font Bureau for two reasons. First, we needed to ensure that the design's original personality remained intact through the delicate updating process. Second, as part of our plan to add new weights, we looked for a partner with deep experience and a reputation for top-quality design work.'

'ITC Franklin Gothic is one of the most well-known and respected faces, particularly in the newspaper industry and advertising markets,' said David Berlow, head designer and co-founder of Font Bureau. 'Designed as a display face, ITC Franklin Gothic was used often over the years for text purposes. Moving forward with ITC, the family will have special display versions and finally a suite of true text fonts, including agate versions for small sizes, such as those used for box scores and stock quotes.'

ITC Franklin is expected to grow to 72 fonts, with the first set of 32 display faces available from www.ITCFonts.com and www.fontbureau.com in 2005. Text and agate weights, available through Font Bureau, will follow later in 2005. The fonts will be offered for both Macintosh and Microsoft Windows platforms in the PostScript, TrueType and OpenType font formats. A suite of alternate characters, simpler access to tabular figures and other features will be included in the OpenType collection.

'The reason to drop "Gothic" from the name boiled down to a practical decision,' Haley said. 'The name was becoming unruly, especially with weights such as ITC Franklin Gothic Extra Condensed Italic. Aside from that, the name Franklin Gothic has always been an anomaly – the face is not a gothic type style, and it also has no relation to Benjamin Franklin, after whom the typeface was named.'

Franklin Gothic was created at the turn of the 20th century by Morris Fuller Benton. The typeface was the third in a series of sans-serif families designed after the American Type Founders was formed in 1892. Released as a single roman weight, additional variants were gradually added, including a condensed in 1905 and an extra-condensed in 1906. An italic weight followed in 1911 and a shaded weight was offered two years later as the last Benton addition to the Franklin Gothic series.

In 1980, ITC revived Franklin Gothic whilst retaining the characteristics of the original typeface. Slight increases were made in the x-height and character width to distinguish the face from Benton's design. 'The general attitude, even among purists, is that ITC Franklin Gothic is a worthy design. It's also one of ITC's best-selling typefaces,' Haley explains.

As part of ITC's collaboration with Font Bureau, the existing ITC Franklin Gothic faces will undergo a 're-envisioning' process, according to Berlow. 'This involves applying modifications to enhance the appearance of the types at larger sizes, then at reading sizes, and then in the agate. This is all accomplished through the subtle manipulation of stroke weights, shapes and the sizes of letters,' Berlow said. 'The professional segment of the publishing market has evolved tremendously since the 80s and early 90s. Publishing experts are able to easily identify the need for and apply enhanced typography, such as these ITC Franklin fonts,' he added.

abcdefghijklm

nopqrstuvwxyz

1234567890

(.,-:;!?'ʻ*[&%§)

A B C D E F G H I

J K L M N O P Q R

S T U V W X Y Z

ITCFranklin-Regular

ITC Franklin – David Berlow – 2004

Font Bureau was founded in 1989 by noted publication designer and consultant Roger Black and type designer David Berlow to serve the emerging needs of microcomputer-based magazine and newspaper publishers seeking unique typographic identities.

The New York Times, *Newsweek* and *Smart* were among the first clients to commission type designs. Since 1995, Font Bureau has designed over 500 fonts for over 100 publications. A few of these designs remain the exclusive property of the publications but most have become part of Font Bureau's retail library.

The library was launched with thirteen fonts and a licensing agreement with FontShop International in 1990. It is now offered directly to end users by Font Bureau and through a select handful of distributors, including FontShop, DSGNHaus, Fontworks UK, Agfa, Precision Type, Phil's Fonts and Atomic Type. The third edition of Font Bureau's specimen book was published in 2001, updating the previous 1997 and 1995 editions.

Font Bureau has also developed OEM* fonts (creating Apple Computer's System 7 and 8), highly specialized fonts for Prodigy Online (Microsoft's applications division), @Home Network online text and display web type and Adobe's most advanced printer solutions. Font Bureau continues to blaze new trails in font formats like TrueTypeTM, fonts for the web and OpenTypeTM.

The company has remained small and privately owned, with freelance and independent designers providing infusions of creativity. The full-time staff has grown to include general manager Sam Berlow, designers and managers Cyrus Highsmith and Jill Pichotta and the sales and marketing team of Samantha Grimsley, Michael Manfredi, Robb Ogle and Harry Parker. A studio located in Boston serves as the company's headquarters.

84 Point   3 A 4a

Sift

QUARTZ
Borough

18 Point   8 A 17 a

NITROGEN
Hymnology

42 Point   5 A 9 a

Magnet

120 Point   3 A 4 a

36 Point   5 A 11 a

Respited

Bait

Demos/Praxis – Gerard Unger – 2004

Gerard Unger was born in Arnhem, the Netherlands, in 1942. He studied graphic design, typography and type design from 1963 to 1967 at the Gerrit Rietveld Academy, Amsterdam. He has worked as a freelance designer since 1975 and, in 1976, his first digital typefaces, Demos and Praxis, were marketed in Germany. Gerard Unger has taught at the Rhode Island School of Design, Providence, USA. He has designed stamps, coins, magazines, newspapers, books, logos, corporate identities, annual reports and many other objects, including a number of type designs. In 1984, he was awarded the H.N. Werkman prize for his typographic work, in particular for digital type designs and for the way he reconciles technology and typographic culture. In 1988, he won the Gravisie prize for the concept behind the face Swift and, in 1991, he was awarded the international Maurits Enschedé-Prize for all his type designs. Beginning in 1987, he served for three years as a jury member for the Dutch Best Designed Books award, during two years of which he was chairman. He teaches as visiting professor at The University of Reading, UK, in the department of typography and graphic communication and part time at the Gerrit Rietveld Academy.

In 1989 and 1990, he wrote a column on typographic topics, called 'The Letter', for the Dutch newspaper Trouw. He has written articles for the trade press and several larger publications, such as Landscape with Letters (1989), linking the usually limited scope of type and typography with a much wider cultural view. In 1995, his book Terwijl je leest (While You Are Reading) – about the reading process – appeared in Dutch, with a German version published in 2003. He lectures frequently in Holland and internationally about his own work, type design, the reading process, newspaper design and related subjects. Fonts by Gerard Unger include: Markeur (1972), M.O.L. (1974), Demos (1976), Demos (new version 2001), Praxis (1977), Hollander (1983), Flora (1984), Swift (1985), Swift 2.0 (1995), Amerigo (1986), Oranda (1987), Argo (1991), Delftse Poort (1991), Decoder (1992), Gulliver (1993), ANWB fonts (1997), Capitolium (1998), Paradox (1999), Coranto (2000), Vesta (2001). Demos (1976) was one of the first digital typefaces. In the Digiset, a composing machine manufactured by Dr-Ing. Rudolf Hell GmbH of Kiel, Germany, letters were formed by a cathode-ray tube and built up from fairly coarse pixels. Photosetting was then still an imperfect technology and Demos was designed to resist such distortion as the rounding of corners during the photographic process. Experiments with counters were carried further with this design. At the same time, Unger was investigating making larger and smaller letters from the same original design. Punch cutters adjusted each size of a letterpress typeface separately by eye. In Demos, there is relatively little difference between thick vertical and thin horizontal parts, facilitating linear enlargement and reduction as type in small sizes is less prone to distortion. In 2001, Demos was redigitized and further refined for use by the German government.

abcdefghijklm

nopqrstuvwxyz

1234567890

(. , - : ; ! ? ' ' * [& % §)

A B C D E F G H I

J K L M N O P Q R

S T U V W X Y Z

aA

Demos

abcdefghijklm

nopqrstuvwxyz

1234567890

(.,-:;!?'''*[&%§)

A B C D E F G H I

J K L M N O P Q R

S T U V W X Y Z

During setting, the letters were drawn with vertical lines formed with a cathode-ray tube. As a result, there were jagged lines, or 'jaggies', in curved lines, which largely disappeared with reductions in size and with the reaction of the printing ink on the paper.

In early digital setting machines, letterforms were stored as a collection of dots. Letter design was based on a grid on which dots were added or deducted using black and white paint.

Proofs of Demos from 1977, where the letters in the title have been narrowed.

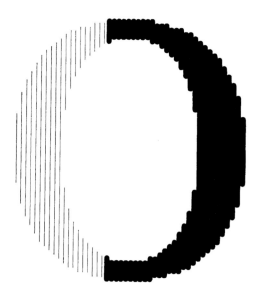

Twee vakbonden zoeken contact met VMF-leiding

Utrecht, 16 april—De Industriebond CNV en de beambtenbond Unie BLHP hebben zich tegenover de raad van bestuur van VMF bereid verklaard het overleg te hervatten over alle problemen, die zich bij het concern voordoen. Als voorwaarde vooral stellen de twee bonden dat bij de plasticmachine-fabriek SPPM in Hengelo een 'zo groot mogelijke werkgelenheid' in stand wordt gehouden. De raad van bestuur staat op het standpunt dat het VMF-bedrijf SPPM moet sluiten.

Brochures that form part of an information campaign by the German Ministry of Transport, Construction and Housing, for which Demos and Praxis were specially modified. The campaign concept and design was by Odeon Zwo, Berlin and Hanover.

FamiliDeutschland

Über 100 Vorteile für das Familienleben

„Die Politik der Regierung ist im Zusammenhang zu sehen. Der erste Schritt war die Steuerentlastung vor allem für Bürger mit niedrigeren Einkommen. Den Abschreibungskünstlern wurden im Gegenzug viele Steuersparmöglichkeiten gestrichen. Jetzt kommt das Sparpaket, in dem es darum geht, den Staatshaushalt zu sanieren. Eine Gerechtigkeitslücke sehe ich nicht."

HUBERTUS SCHMOLDT

Vorsitzender der IG-BCE, in: „Wirtschaftswoche" vom 30/9/1999

DIE GRUNDLAGEN: 21

Zukunftsprogramm kann nur mit einer großen Kraftanstrengung auf den Weg gebracht werden. Es schafft die Basis, um wieder **mehr Spielraum für Zukunftsinvestitionen**, für die Sicherung unseres Sozialsystems und für die weitere Verbesserung der wirtschaftlichen Rahmenbedingungen zu gewinnen. Das ist der richtige Kurs für soziale Gerechtigkeit, Wohlstand und vor allem mehr Arbeitsplätze.

„The new categorical imperative: Live your life in a way that could be conveyed to all people to the world!"

Jochen Flasbarth, Regulatory Association for the Protection of Nature of Germany (NABU e. V.)

Politics
by c o m m i t m e n t

Respect, care and responsibility · these are the intrinsic ethical values that our friendships, families and communities are built on and at the same time they represent what sustainability means in our relationship with nature and the future generations.

Appointed in April 2001 by **Chancellor Gerhard Schröder, the German Council for Sustainable Development** is an independent political advisory to the Federal Government and especially to the Green Cabinet, an interdepartmental steering group set up to draft the national sustainability strategy.

„A Germany that is sustainable means: Protecting our natural foundations of life also for f u t u r e generations with maximised economic growth."

Prof. Dr. Wolfgang Franz, President of the Centre for European Economic Research (ZEW), Mannheim

Digital font technology allowed Hermann Zapf to realize a dream he first had more than fifty years ago: to create a fully calligraphic typeface. Zapf began work on Zapfino in 1993, in technical collaboration with David Siegel and Gino Lee, who were responsible for the initial digitization.

The first PostScript and TrueType versions were completed and released by Linotype Library GmbH as a set of six fonts.

The Zapfino fonts consist of four basic alphabets, with many additional stylistic alternatives that can be freely mixed together to emulate the variations in handwritten text.

Its introduction into the market had an auspicious start and the Type Directors Club of New York has presented Linotype Zapfino with the prestigious TDC Type Design Award.

a b c d e f g h i j k l m

n o p q r s t u v w x y z

1 2 3 4 5 6 7 8 9 0

(. , - : ; ! ? ' ` * I @ % §)

y y v f f f

A B C D E F G H I

J K L M N O P Q R

S T U V W X Y Z

LTZapfino One

Wie kann man bei der Wahl schwanken,
ob man sein Leben den Frauen oder den Büchern weihen soll!
Kann man eine Frau, wenn sie ihre Launen hat,
zuklappen und ins Regal stellen?
Wanderte schon einmal ein Buch, ohne dich zu fragen,
einfach aus deinem Zimmer weg in den Bücherschrank eines anderen?
Hat je ein Buch, stand dir gerade die Lust zu einem anderen,
wolltest du schlafen oder auch nichts tun,
von dir verlangt, du solltest gerade jetzt es lesen
und ihm allein dich widmen? Werden die Suppen von Büchern versalzen?
Können Bücher schmollen, Klavier spielen?
Einen Mangel freilich haben sie: sie können nicht küssen!
Hans von Weber

The very first sketches of a calligraphic
script by Hermann Zapf, Bordeaux
1944. Some years later these became
the source of Zapfino.

Sketches of the so-called 'Hyper-
Swashes', 1977.

Pages 116–17: Drawings for Zapfino.

ABCDEFGHIJKLMN

Small caps for Zapfino

OPQRSTUVWXYZ

Special big descenders and ascenders
(will be reduced for Linotype specifications)

ÆØ

V

ELN

if wanted also swash initials
for small caps

g

g

h

Z 1997

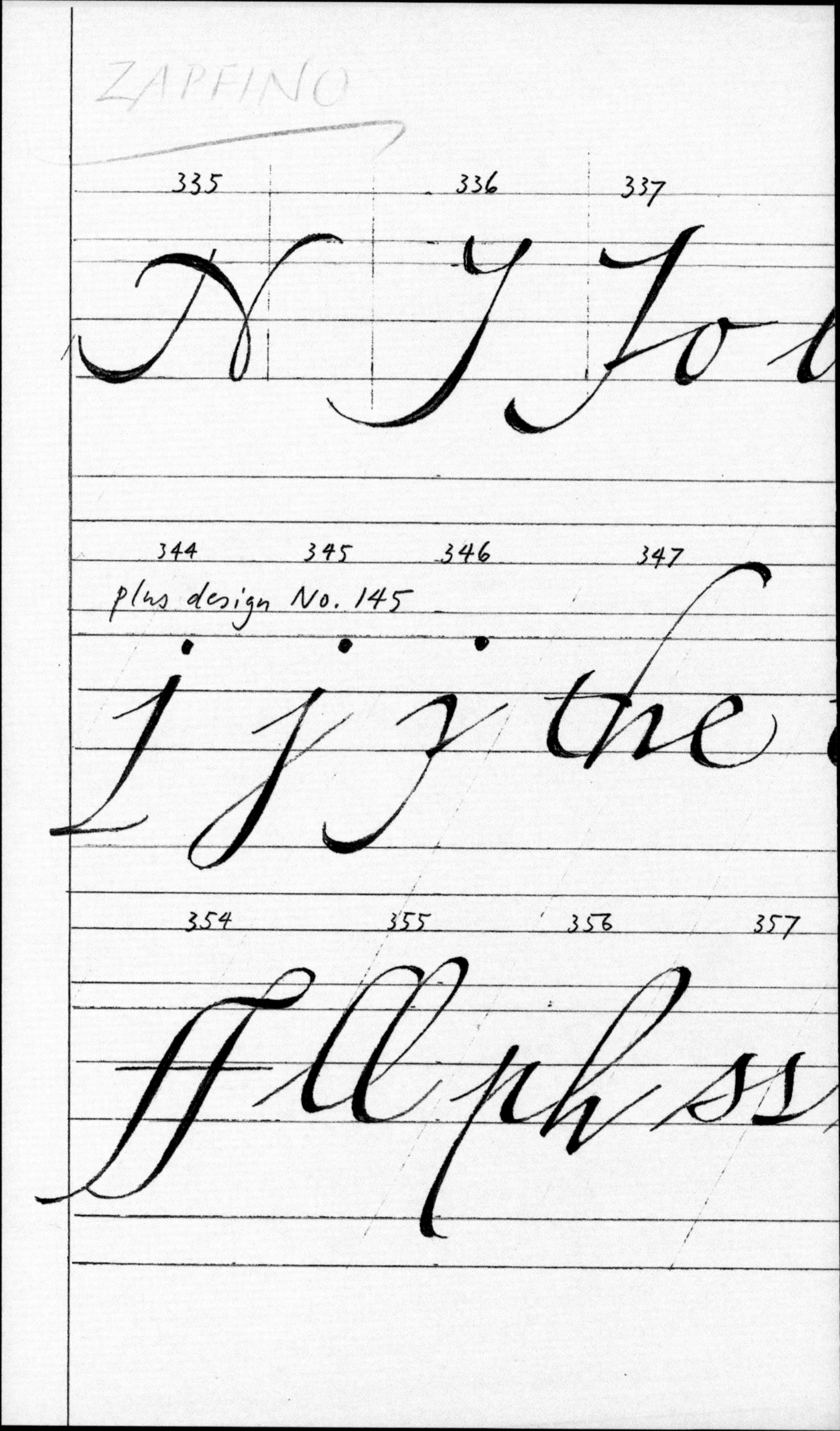

ZAPFINO

335　　　　　　336　　　337

N T To

344　　　345　　346　　　347

plus design No. 145

j j j the

354　　　　355　　　356　　　357

ff Al ph ss

338	339	340	341	342	343

b S S 8 4 3

348	349	350	351	352

353

he 3 G ffir

358	359	360	361

sh the ppa

117

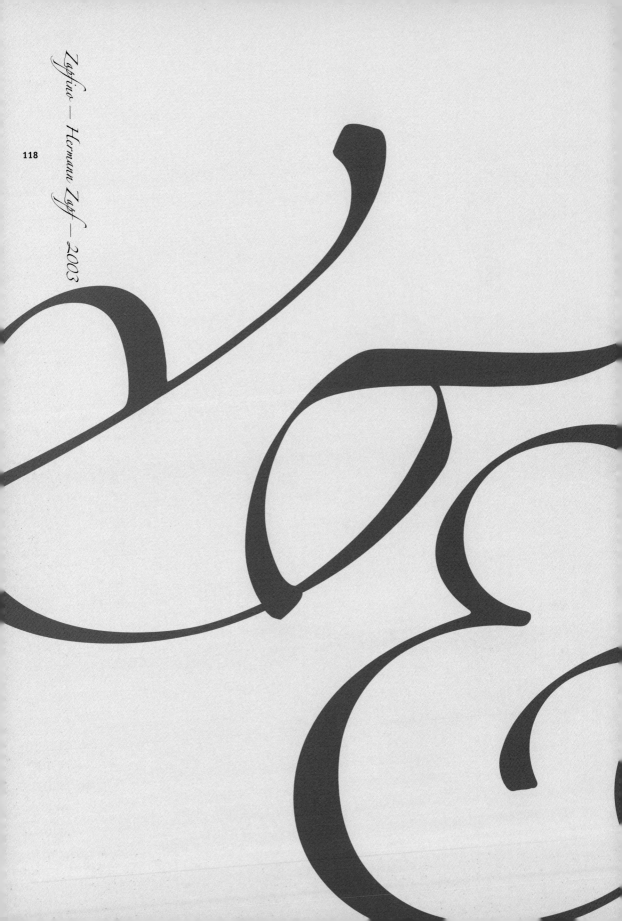

118

Erik van Blokland (1967) and Just van Rossum (1966) 'work apart together' in their partnership and have been each other's sounding board for many years under the joint label of LettError. Each has his own clients and individual fortes. They both studied at The Hague Royal Academy (KABK) and were influenced by Gerrit Noordzij, and, after graduating, they worked in Berlin at Erik Spiekermann's MetaDesign.

Two typefaces, Beowolf (1990) and Twin (2003), were designed jointly.

For both Van Blokland and Van Rossum, a font is a software instruction to a printer to perform a task. When using PostScript fonts (developed by Adobe), the typefaces are specifically digitized. The duo 'hacked' PostScript by adding a new function, named 'freakto', and the result was Times New Random, later renamed Beowolf, a typeface that changes while it is being printed. No two shapes are identical. The dynamics of letterpress generated by digital means.

With his typeface Kosmik, Erik van Blokland put a new digital invention into practice: the 'flipperfont', a tiny program embedded in the font that ensures the printer randomly selects one of three available versions of each character. Van Blokland based Kosmik on the hand-drawn letters he used in his comic strips. Van Blokland and Van Rossum have been commissioned to produce custom typefaces for such clients as GAK (the Dutch government agency for the administration of national insurance), MTV Europe and MTV UK. They are two typeface designers with the talent and skill to conjure up impeccable typographic creations.

a b c d e f g h i j k l m

n o p q r s t u v w x y z

1 2 3 4 5 6 7 8 9 0

(. , - : ; ! ? ' ' * [& % §)

A B C D E F G H I

J K L M N O P Q R

S T U V W X Y Z

A A A

Kosmik-PlainOne

FF Kosmik OT
Autofflippperr*
01234567890123456789
Plain & **Bold** ¶ ✈ ⊕
✽In OpenType Savvy Applications
Liveliness, Onomatopaea
MACOS+WIN, SCREEN+PRINT
OpenTypeFontFont

Then, all of a sudden, Typoman remembered! It's Flippers! FF Kosmik is alive...

MMM
MMM
MMM
MMM
MMM

Beowolf breaks all
the rules; it looks
different each time
you use it.

Fontshops Beowolf jumps over the lazy dog
and changes all experience of fonts
1234567890
Fontshops Beowolf jumps over the lazy dog
and changes all experience of fonts
1234567890

Jetzt gibt es eine
Schrift, die aussieht,
wie von Hand
skizziert, obwohl sie
aus dem Computer
stammt. Beowolf von
FontShop

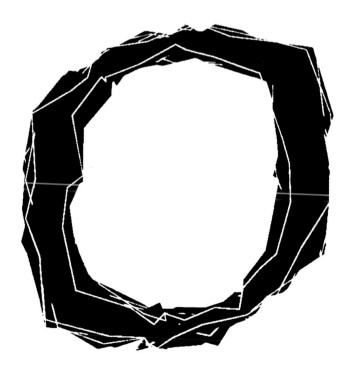

ABCDEFGHIJK
LMNOPQRST
UVWXYZ
1234567890
&
abcdefghijklmn
opqrstuvwxyz
-.,.:;!?„"''‚"–

MONA LISA

Beowolf was
computerized in
the early stages
of its design using
Ikarus M. The
finishing touches
were applied
on screen.

AntwortFax der Original BeowolfRandomDesigners! Idee: Erik van Blokland und Just van Rossum (1989) Schrift: Gestaltung Erik van Blokland (1988) Programm: IkarusM und dann von Hand in der PostScript code gehackt. Andere Schriften lassen sich erstmal nicht ändern, aber wir arbeiten dran. Die Schrift wird gekauft von vielen Leuten die interessiert sind an Typografie, und bereit sind das Abenteuer der RandomFonts an zu geben. Die Fonts sind da um gegen die allgemeine Glattheit der Adobe u.ä. Fonts ein Gegengewicht zu setzen. Nah, ein Zielgruppe gibt's eigentlich nicht- oder vielleicht Leute mit Macintosh Computers und Laserdrucker, die etwas von Typo wissen.

Nutzen? RandomFonts sehen einfach gut aus, und machen Riesenspaß beim Farb-trennung weil jede Farbe anders wird. Das offizielle FontShop Zahl zur RandomFont verkauf ist 20. (das kann ja aber auch ziemlich zufällig sein) grüß Erik van Blokland+Just van Rossum, FontShop

abcdefghijklmnopqrstuvwxyz

ABCDEFGHIJKLMNOPQRSTUVWXYZ

ABCDEFGHIJKMNOPQRSTUVXYZ

«(¶ae ffffiffifilist&ctflfflftThrn§]*

£0123456789 &0123456789€

SABON NEXT BY JEAN FRANÇOIS PORCHEZ

£0123456789 & 0123456789$

«(¶ae ffffiffifilistQ&AflfflftThrv§}*

ABCDEFGHIJKMNOPQRSTUVXYZ

ABCDEFGHIJKLMNOPQRSTUVWXYZ

abcdefghijklmnopqrstuvwxyz

After training as a graphic designer, specializing in type design, Jean François Porchez (b. 1964) worked as a type director at Dragon Rouge. By 1994, he had created the new typeface for *Le Monde* newspaper. Today, he designs custom typefaces for companies such as RATP (Public Transport in Paris), Peugeot, Costa Crocieres and France Télécom, as well as internationally distributing his retail typefaces on his typofonderie.com website. For the Linotype Library Platinum Collection, he produced a revival of Sabon, which was, in turn, a Jan Tschichold revival of Garamond. Porchez was a jury member at the 3rd Linotype Type Design Contest and is vice president of ATypI. He teaches type design at ENSAD (France) and is a visiting lecturer on the typeface design MA course at The University of Reading (UK). Porchez also contributes regularly to conferences and international publications and has published *Lettres Françaises*, a book (in French and English) that shows all contemporary French digital typefaces. In late 2001, he was the president of a jury set up by the French Ministry of Education to select the new handwriting model and system for France. Porchez was awarded the Charles Peignot prize in 1998. FF Angie (1990) and Apolline (1993) were prize-winning entries in the Morisawa typeface competition. The Costa font received a Certificate of Excellence in Type Design at the TDC2 2000. Ambroise, Anisette, Anisette Petite, Charente, Le Monde Journal and Le Monde Courrier were all prize-winning entries in the Bukvaraz international competition (2001).

Typefaces to date: Angie (1990), Angie Sans (1994), Apolline (1993), Le Monde (1994), Le Monde Sans (1994), Anisette (1995), Parisine (2 series, 1996), Le Monde Journal (1997), Le Monde Sans (1997), Le Monde Livre (1997), Le Monde Courrier (1997), Sitaline (1998), Lion (1999), Parisine (complete, 1999), Costa (1999), Parisine Plus (1999), Le Monde Livre Classic (1999), Charente (2000), Bienvenue (2000), Ambroise (2001), Anisette Petite (2001), Marianne (2002), Sabon Next (2002).

abcdefghijklm

nopqrstuvwxyz

1234567890

(. , - : ; ! ? ' ' * [& % §)

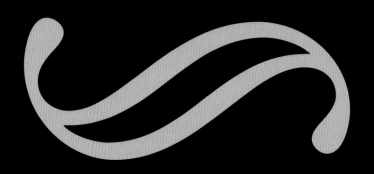

ABCDEFGHI

JKLMNOPQR

STUVWXYZ

Sabon Next LT Regular

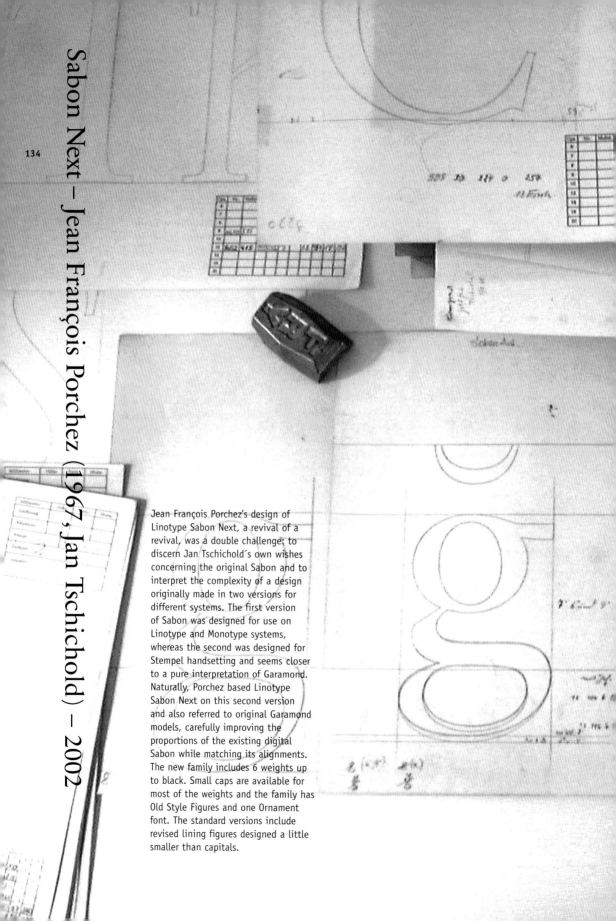

Sabon Next – Jean François Porchez (1967, Jan Tschichold) – 2002

Jean François Porchez's design of
Linotype Sabon Next, a revival of a
revival, was a double challenge: to
discern Jan Tschichold's own wishes
concerning the original Sabon and to
interpret the complexity of a design
originally made in two versions for
different systems. The first version
of Sabon was designed for use on
Linotype and Monotype systems,
whereas the second was designed for
Stempel handsetting and seems closer
to a pure interpretation of Garamond.
Naturally, Porchez based Linotype
Sabon Next on this second version
and also referred to original Garamond
models, carefully improving the
proportions of the existing digital
Sabon while matching its alignments.
The new family includes 6 weights up
to black. Small caps are available for
most of the weights and the family has
Old Style Figures and one Ornament
font. The standard versions include
revised lining figures designed a little
smaller than capitals.

Sabon Next – Jean François Porchez (1967, Jan Tschichold) – 2002

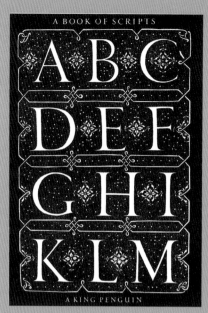

A BOOK OF SCRIPTS

ABC DEF GHI KLM

A KING PENGUIN

Left: Cover design for *A book of Scripts* by Alfred Fairbank, Penguin Books, adapted by Jan Tschichold in 1949 from a design by Juan de Ycìar in 1547.

Below: Cover for a printer in Leipzig, Germany, 1923, which shows Tschichold's own calligraphy based on Renaissance models.

Bottom: Sabon Next refers to original Garamond models, carefully improving the proportions of the existing digital Sabon.

Opposite: Jean François Porchez, cover, 2002.

FISCHER & WITTIG
Buchdruckerei und Buchbinderei
LEIPZIG

Herstellung aller
buchgewerblichen Erzeugnisse in
erstklassiger Ausführung

EIGENER POSTKARTENVERLAG

Zur Leipziger Messe:
Bugra-Messe · Petersstraße 38·1
und im Hause Grimmaische Str. 26· Hof rechts·

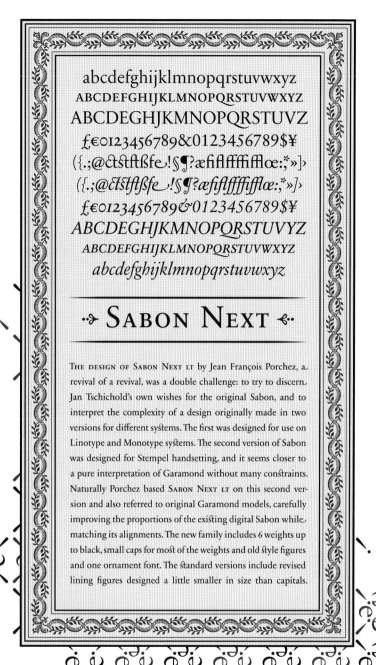

abcdefghijklmnopqrstuvwxyz
ABCDEFGHIJKLMNOPQRSTUVWXYZ
ABCDEGHJKMNOPQRSTUVZ
ſ€0123456789&0123456789$¥
({.;@ctstſtßfe‿!§¶?æfiflﬀﬃﬄﬀﬂœ:;*»]›
({.;@ctstſtßfe‿!§¶?æfiflﬀﬃﬄﬀﬂœ:;*»]›
ſ€0123456789&0123456789$¥
ABCDEGHJKMNOPQRSTUVYZ
ABCDEFGHIJKLMNOPQRSTUVWXYZ
abcdefghijklmnopqrstuvwxyz

⤙ SABON NEXT ⤚

THE DESIGN OF SABON NEXT LT by Jean François Porchez, a
revival of a revival, was a double challenge: to try to discern
Jan Tschichold's own wishes for the original Sabon, and to
interpret the complexity of a design originally made in two
versions for different systems. The first was designed for use on
Linotype and Monotype systems. The second version of Sabon
was designed for Stempel handsetting, and it seems closer to
a pure interpretation of Garamond without many constraints.
Naturally Porchez based SABON NEXT LT on this second version and also referred to original Garamond models, carefully
improving the proportions of the existing digital Sabon while
matching its alignments. The new family includes 6 weights up
to black, small caps for most of the weights and old style figures
and one ornament font. The standard versions include revised
lining figures designed a little smaller in size than capitals.

POÈME PANCARTE

✳

par ici ——————— ☞

☞ ——————— par là

1 KM. 500

PARADIS

✳

*suivez jusqu'au bout
ensuite vous demanderez aux anges.*

D'après Pierre-Albert Birot.

"*leet us at bett sexy*"

☞ **CG + JT + JFP = JAZZTYPE FROM 10PM**

if

W
Y
S
I
WYG

ah… **l'or**

LEONARDO SIMEO
CARLO & LEA

2

 L'hypocrisie est
un hommage
que le vice
rend à la vertu.

kunst macht frei

RAPPELLE-TOI QU'IL FAUT SUIVRE

LA
MODE
TYPOGRAPHIQUE

Souvenir des
CALANQUES
de Piana,
haut lieu
du tourisme
Corse

Qui vit content de peu possède tout.

Dis peu

Jean François Porchez,
revival of Sabon, 2002.

nandnenon

nandnenon

haRGfrépgE

haRGfrepgE

Le Monde
Le Monde
Le Monde
Le Monde
Le Monde
Le Monde
Le Monde
Le Monde
Le Monde
Le Monde
Le Monde
Le Monde
Le Monde
Le Monde
Le Monde
Le Monde
Le Monde
Le Monde
Le Monde
Le Monde
Le Monde
Le Monde
Le Monde
Le Monde
Le Monde
Le Monde
Le Monde
Le Monde
Le Monde
Le Monde
Le Monde
Le Monde
Le Monde
Le Monde
Le Monde
Le Monde
Le Monde

Capitales plus petites. *Smaller capitals.*　Empattements décalés. *Gap serifs.*　Horizontales affirmées. *Strong horizontality.*　Contre-formes plus ouvertes. *Open counterforms.*

HOphagnef
HOphagnef

Empattements plus contrastés. *Contrasted serifs.*　Pente moins forte. *Lesser slope.*

Formes plus découpées. *Contrasted forms.*　Empattements simplifiés. *Simplified serifs.*

LE MONDE IS ACTUALLY a set of four typefaces (Le Monde Journal, Le Monde Livre, Le Monde Sans and Le Monde Courrier) that evolved from a design for the famous French newspaper of the same name. **In both instances** Porchez is working within the narrow area of type design that involves readability, legibility and ergonomics. *These typefaces are subtle variations on familiar themes rather than part of the contemporary typographic free-for-all.* Le Monde Journal, the original member of the Le Monde quartet, was designed for the newspaper when it was in the midst of a financial crisis in early 1994. Porchez read about Le Monde's "last chance redesign" and decided to propose a new typeface, one that would be both more readable as well as better adapted to both French culture and modern methods of printing. He made a

LE MONDE IS ACTUALLY a set of four typefaces (Le Monde Journal, Le Monde Livre, Le Monde Sans and Le Monde Courrier) that evolved from a design for the famous French newspaper of the same name. **In both instances** Porchez is working within the narrow area of type design that involves readability, legibility and ergonomics. *These typefaces are subtle variations on familiar themes rather than part of the contemporary typographic free-for-all.* Le Monde Journal, the original member of the Le Monde quartet, was designed for the newspaper when it was in the midst of a financial crisis in early 1994. Porchez read about Le Monde's "last chance redesign" and decided to propose a new typeface, one that would be both more readable as well as better adapted to both French culture and modern methods of printing. He made a

LE MONDE IS ACTUALLY a set of four typefaces (Le Monde Journal, Le Monde Livre, Le Monde Sans and Le Monde Courrier) that evolved from a design for the famous French newspaper of the same name. **In both instances** Porchez is working within the narrow area of type design that involves readability, legibility and ergonomics. *These typefaces are subtle variations on familiar themes rather than part of the contemporary typographic free-for-all.* Le Monde Journal, the original member of the Le Monde quartet, was designed for the newspaper when it was in the midst of a financial crisis in early 1994. Porchez read about Le Monde's "last chance redesign" and decided to propose a new typeface, one that would be both more readable as well as better adapted to both French culture and modern methods

LE MONDE IS ACTUALLY a set of four typefaces (Le Monde Journal, Le Monde Livre, Le Monde Sans and Le Monde Courrier) that evolved from a design for the famous French newspaper of the same name. **In both instances** Porchez is working within the narrow area of type design that involves readability, legibility and ergonomics. *These typefaces are subtle variations on familiar themes rather than part of the contemporary typographic free-for-all.* Le Monde Journal, the original member of the Le Monde quartet, was designed for the newspaper when it was in the midst of a financial crisis in early 1994. Porchez read about Le Monde's "last chance redesign" and decided to propose a new typeface, one that would be both more readable as well as better adapted to both French culture and modern methods

abcdefghijklm

nopqrstuvwxyz

1 2 3 4 5 6 7 8 9 0

(. , - : ; ! ? ' ' * [& % §)

A B C D E F G H I

J K L M N O P Q R

S T U V W X Y Z

LeMonde Journal

L'Illustration

Grande Mobilisation !

AFFAIRE TRÈS EUROPÉENNE

Journaux

Prise de la Tour de Malakoff

dʒupm̥aʃ

θmeçbaɣn ŋl ɔ̃ɡuicç

Beau Garage

not monospaced

Courriers

Chère grand-mère, nos vacances se passent bien

Letter setting

typewritten

La chaise

LE BULLETIN

Un traité d'art décoratif

Rhinocéros fou

À titre indicatif, 3500 F DONNE 530,30 €

La belle Italique

L'année dernière, j'ai lu 2467 romans

Some books on Type

finer French type cast by Mathis Porchez

Renaissance du livre

26 caractères

Les Classiques

finer French type cast by Mathis Porchez

LA TYPO & TES CARACTÈRES

Ligatures

Le Monde – Jean François Porchez – 1997

Porchez presents four fonts – Le Monde Journal, Le Monde Livre, Le Monde Sans and Le Monde Courrier – in the pages of this book. The fonts are named after the famous French newspaper *Le Monde*.

abcdefghijklmnopq
rstuvwxyzæœfiflffffi
fflß&ABCDEFGHIJKL
MNOPQRSTUVWXYZ
ÆŒ&ABCDEFGHI
JKLMNOPQRSTUV
WXYZÆŒ01234567
89$¢£¥€ƒ012345678
9$¢£¥€ƒ0123456789-
-–—!?(|)•[/]\{/}«‹.,""@

abcdefghijklmnopqrs
tuvwxyzæœfiflffffiﬄﬂß
&ABCDEFGHIJKLMNOP
QRSTUVWXYZÆŒ&AB
CDEFGHIJKLMNOP
QRSTUVWXYZÆŒ0
123456789$¢£¥€ƒ012
3456789$¢£¥€ƒ0123
456789-–—!?(|)•[/]\{/
}«‹.,""'@%#†§¶ªº°®*

R

N

X

Hans Eduard Meier was born in Horgen am Zürichsee, Switzerland, in 1922. After studying at the Zurich design school, he embarked on a career as a graphic designer, working in Zurich and Paris for such clients as UNESCO. In 1959, his trilingual text book, *Der Schriftentwicklung (The Evolution of Typography)*, was published and the eleventh edition was issued in 1995. He worked with Stempel in the late 1960s, creating that most humanist of sans serifs, Syntax, a type whose influence is clear in Erik Spiekermann's Meta and its followers. In 1984, Meier set up a programme for designing typefaces on the computer with the Institute for Computer Systems at the technical university in Zurich. This collaboration generated the Barbedor, Syndor and Oberon fonts and, also, Barbetwo, Syntax-Letter and Lapidar for use within the university. Meier taught typeface design and graphic art at the Kunstgewerbeschule in Zurich for 36 years.

Although he retired in 1986, he continues to design new typefaces and publish them through the Elsner-Flake Digital Library: ABCSchrift Drei EF, ABCSchrift Eins EF, ABCSchrift Zwei EF, Barbedor, BasisSchrift Eins EF, Elysa EF, ITC Syndor, Syntax, Linotype Syntax Lapidar. Barbedor was designed for Hell Digiset in 1984 and is based on the handwritten humanistic book scripts of the 15th century, with figures resembling those written with a broad-tipped pen. Tiny serif-like elements reveal the line of the writing utensil and emphasize the style of the face; classic and legible, Barbedor is a clear, harmonious typeface, an excellent choice for long texts. Its large selection of weights offers a variety of design applications.

Syntax was developed in 1968 and published by the D. Stempel AG type foundry. Meier's basic idea was to create a sans-serif version of Jan Tschichold's Sabon. The result was a revolutionary letterform, initially not accepted by typographers. Its figures are based on Old Face characters but have a distinctive, modern look and the 2° inclination to the right lends the font a dynamic feel. It was first published in 5 different weights: roman, italic, bold, black and ultra-black. In 2000, Meier reworked Syntax into a complete font family, available as Linotype Syntax, exclusively from Linotype Library. The new family consists of light, regular, medium, bold, heavy and black. All weights are also available in italic and many weights are available with small caps and Old Style figures.

abcdefghijklm

nopqrstuvwxyz

1234567890

(.,-:;!?'''*[&%§)

A B C D E F G H I

J K L M N O P Q R

S T U V W X Y Z

RNX

LTSyntax Regular

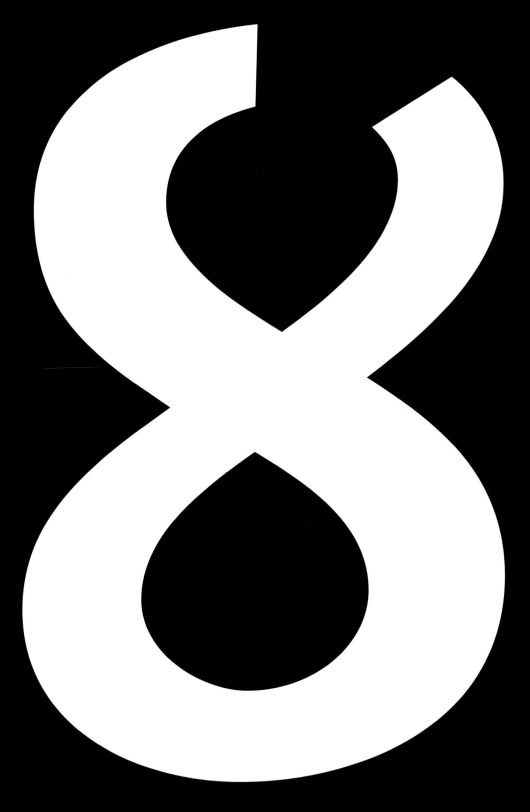

ABCDEFGHIJKLMN
OPQRSTUVWXY
1234567890
abcdefghiklmnopqrs
tuvwxyz Syntax

*ABCDEFGHIJKLMNO
PQRSTUVWXY
1234567890
abcdefghiklmnopqrst
uvwxyz Syntax*

ABCDEFGHIJKLMN
OPQRSTUVWXYZ
1234567890
abcdefghiklmnopqrs
tuvwxyz SyntaxSerif

*ABCDEFGHIJKLMN
OPQRSTUVWXYZ
1234567890
abcdefghiklmnopqrst
uvwxyz SyntaxSerif*

Linotype-Syntax

My first drawings were made in 1955 as I did not like the geometric, technically functioning Grotesque fonts common at that time. I based my designs on the highly legible font Renaissance Antiqua. Studying the handwritten Renaissance, which was the model for the first type settings, made me aware of how printed fonts of our time had become technical and formalist and, therefore, unsuitable as a comfortably readable font for all applications. What was needed was the highly legible Antiqua faces from past centuries.
My new font had to be both modern and legible, like an Antiqua face. It was produced between 1968 and 1972 for both handsetting and Linotype under the name of Syntax at the D. Stempel font foundry. Nowadays, its digital form is available from the Linotype Library. In 1990, I reworked the poorly digitized font on the computer and added new elements. The font was christened by the then artistic director of the foundry, Erich Schulz-Anker. Copyright is owned by Linotype Library.

Linotype-SyntaxSerif

It seemed appropriate to design an Antiqua with proportions, bolds and tracking that fitted in with Syntax. The tracking, flow and weight are identical in both faces. They are also mutually interchangeable. SyntaxSerif was created in 1999. The licensing rights are owned by Linotype Library.

ABCDEFGHIJKLMNO
PQRSTUVWXYZ
1234567890
abcdefghiklmnopqrst
uvwxyz SyntaxLetter

ABCDEFGHIJKLMNO
PQRSTUVWXYZ
1234567890
abcdefghiklmnopqrst
uvwxyz SyntaxLetter I.

ΛBCDEFGHIJKLMN
OPQRSTUVWXY123
4567890
ΛBCDEFÇHIKLMNO
PQRSTUVWXYZ

ΛBCDEFGHIJKLMNO
PQRSTUVWXY
1234567890
ΛbcdEFÇHiklmNopq
rstuvwxyz

Linotype-SyntaxLetter

I designed this face in 1994, when I was fed up with all the letters I received printed in Helvetica or Times, which I do not consider suitable for letters. The faces available were, I felt, too rigid and inappropriate for business correspondence. I was looking for a form close to that of a printed font but based on letters written by hand with a felt-tip pen. This generated a family of fonts similar in scope to Syntax, but which lends itself to more applications than just letters. The licensing rights are owned by Linotype Library.

Syntax-Lapidar Display and Text

The dynamism of a face hewn from stone in 2A.D. inspired me in 1995 to design a complete font on the computer. It differs distinctly from the Roman faces of 2A.D., which were designed in accordance with the architectonic principle that the foundation of a letter should be slightly larger than the upper part (B, E, H, K, R, S, X and so forth). Lapidar Display is made up entirely of capitals, with variations on the capitals used instead of lowercase letters.

ΛBCDEFGHIJKLMN
OPQRSTUVWXY123
4567890
ΛBCDEFÇHIKLMNOP
QRSTUVWXYZ

ΛBCDEFGHIJKLMN
OPQRSTUVWXY
1234567890
Λbcdefçhiklmnopq
rstuvwxyz

ABCDEFGHIJKLMNOP
QRSTUVWXYZ
1234567890
abcdefghiklmnopqrstu
vwxyz ITC-Syndor

ABCDEFGHIJKLMNOPQ
RSTUVWXYZ
1234567890
abcdefghiklmnopqrstuv
wxyz ITC-Syndor Italic

Syntax-Lapidar Serif Display and Text

Ancient serif examples of the Lapidar face prompted me to add serifs to Lapidar in 2000. The angular serifs support the dynamism of the font. The licensing rights are owned by Linotype Library.

Syntax-Lapidar Text

For lowercase letters, Lapidar has elements that resemble a capital-like character. The dimensions of these lowercase letters correspond with the ratio between the small and large letters in a normal face. Licensing rights are owned by Linotype Library.

ITC-Syndor

Created in 1992, this font unites the characteristics of Syntax and Barbedor. Syntax has now been given serifs, not the usual serifs, but more like those in Barbedor, although far more obvious. In addition to the traits borrowed from Syntax and Barbedor, Syndor also has its own independent character. The licensing rights are owned by ITC-Agfa-Monotype in Wilmington, USA.

ABCDEFGHIJKLMNOP
QRSTUVWXYZ
1234567890
abcdefghiklmnopqrstu
vwxyz Barbedor

ABCDEFGHIJKLMNOP
QRSTUVWXYZ
1234567890
abcdefghiklmnopqrstuv
wxyz Barbedor Italic

ABCDEFGHIJKLMNOPQ
RSTUVWXYZ
1234567890
abcdefghiklmnopqrstu
vwxyz? Oberon

ABCDEFGHIJKLMNOPQRS
TUVWXYZ
1234567890
abcdefghiklmnopqrstuv
wxyz? Oberon Italic

Barbedor

In 1984, I had the chance to learn computer-aided letter design at the Institute for Computer Systems in Zurich's technical university. I took advantage of the opportunity to use the handwritten face Antiqua, based on the faces of the Renaissance, as a model for a printed font. Unlike Syntax, which is also based on Antiqua's basic form, Barbedor adheres strictly to Antiqua's written form. I named the font after the famous calligrapher Barbedor, who lived in Paris in the 17th century. Licensing rights are owned by Elsner-Flake GbR, Hamburg.

Oberon

Oberon is closely related to Syndor, however, the strong stroke endings are more horizontal, giving the face a restful look. Licensing rights are owned by Elsner-Flake GbR, Hamburg.

ABCDEFGHIJKLMNOP
QRSTUVWXYZ
1234567890
abcdefghiklmnopqrst
uvwxyz

ABCDEFGHIJKLMNOP
QRSTUVWXYZ
1234567890
abcdefghiklmnopqrstu
vwxyz

ABCDEFGHIJKLMNO
PQRSTUVWXYZ
1234567890
abcdefghiklmnopqrstuv
wxyz

ABCDEFGHIJKLMN
OPQRSTUVWXYZ
1234567890
abcdefghijklmn
opqrstuvwxzy

Elysa

Barbedor, my first computer-aided font design, had a few shortcomings. I had to admit that it is impossible to use a form written entirely as if by quill as a printing font. The extremely fine handwritten parts were disturbing and looked grainy at small point sizes. In 2002, I expanded Barbedor, renaming it Elysa, and added Swash letters with several variations and the appropriate ornaments. Licensing rights are owned by Elsner-Flake GbR, Hamburg.

ABCDEFGHIJKLMNO
PQRSTUVWX YZ
1234567890
abcde fghi kl
m n opgr s

ABCDEFGHIJKLMNOPQ
RSTUVWXYZ
1234567890
abcdefghiklmnopqrstu
uwxyz

ABCDEFGHIJKLMNOPQ
RSTUVWXYZ
1234567890
abcdefghiklmnopqrstu
uwxyz

ABC-Schulschrift

It had been bothering me for some time that the Swiss *Schnürlischrift* had been taught as the compulsory handwriting style to Swiss school children since 1947. Granted, today it is no longer compulsory but, in the absence of a better alternative, it is still taught. As this also displeased a number of teachers, I started designing a contemporary handwriting style for schools in 2002.

ABC-Schulschrift consists of three alphabets: ABC1, without loops, resembles a Grotesque and is taught to children in their first year of school; ABC2 has the beginnings of loops; and ABC3 is written joined. All three also exist in italic. I wrote an accompanying text book and, with the help of teachers who were already teaching my new hand to their pupils, I developed some worksheets. In the Swiss districts of Glarus and Basel Stadt, my new hand is being taught and I often participate in the lessons. Licensing rights are owned by Elsner-Flake GbR, Hamburg.

ABCDEFGHIJKLMNOPQ
RSTUVWXYZ
1234567890
abcdefghiklmnopqrst
uvwxyz

ABCDEFGHIJKLMNOPQ
RSTUVWXYZ
1234567890
abcdefghiklmnopqrst
uvwxyz

ABCDEFGHIJKLMNOPQR
STUVWXYZ
1234567890
abcdefghiklmnopqrst
uvwxyz

ABCDEFGHIJKLMNOPQ
RSTUVWXYZ
1234567890
abcdefghiklmnopqrs
tuvwxyz

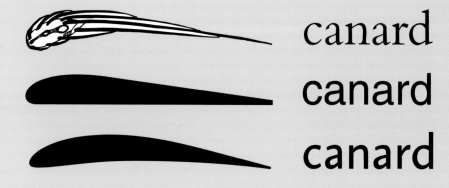

canard

canard

canard

Born in Heidelberg in 1976, Tim Ahrens studied architecture at the University of Karlsruhe from 1997 to 2003. He has published one typeface so far: the sans-serif text face Linotype Aroma.

Ahrens explains, 'I started designing this typeface about six months after learning that Frutiger is not a brand of sweets and that Garamond is not the name of a fragrance. In time it became clear that designing a sans serif should always be considered as a transformation of traditional serif typefaces and not a derivation of typefaces that have been derived from others that have been derived from yet others.

I did not want Aroma to be one of those odourless and tasteless typefaces that sacrifice a natural feel and neutralize the characteristic shapes of the letters.

I think beauty often evolves unintentionally. I am fascinated, for example, by the beauty of aerofoils, which are actually a meticulous derivation of a bird's wing. I love their inorganic, abstract shape, which still bears the essence and the complexity of what they are modelled on. This is exactly the formal concept behind Aroma.

Many of the outlines are actually parabolic. The lowercase "r", for example, consists exclusively of straight lines and parabolae. I decided to give Aroma more stroke contrast than is usual for sans-serif designs, and many strokes are slightly convex, giving the font an inorganic look.

The font was intended to have a similar feel to Antiqua. More specifically, it is based on Old Style faces. The character of those fonts, which were cut during the Renaissance, is still inherent in Aroma.'

abcdefghijklm

nopqrstuvwxyz

1 2 3 4 5 6 7 8 9 0

(. , - : ; ! ? ' ' * [& % §)

A B C D E F G H I

J K L M N O P Q R

S T U V W X Y Z

pfg

LTAroma

Aroma – Tim Ahrens – 1999

ride variety try to think about to when you allow it to move across your
m, apple, bowmores up to 27 range of noses flavour of swallow. Take not
nce sip of the *When I'm working on a* dries or even
nen it first slowly burns the inside in taste from range long-lasting. Tongu
sweet or *problem, I never think about* smoky sn
release the includes come aroma, and palates – from sweet and how th
Eat take a prickles, spoonful of of y
also, you certain enters your mou

beauty.

om mellow and softly warm to strong even bread, whisky. Vanilla, sherry,
d chocolate, *But when I have finished,* caramel and
ing whether the aroma find be called a harmony of easily distinguish the
racteristics, such *if the solution is not* as a flowery, only
h the stems on. Swirl the to be known as for growing the because finest
to judge *beautiful, I know it is wrong* the snack
th or without a could never sour. Amalfi lemons emanate they have a arc
taste, other lemons in 650 g markets because they are the these lemons
fi coastlines R. BUCKMINSTER FULLER terraced gr
t soil biologically without chemical manures or other can easily be enjoy
fashioned natural recipe like natural vanilla. Especially comforting on col

Different applications of Aroma,
showing, for example, a letter's
ascenders or descenders.

Gianotten – Antonio Pace (1970, Giambattista Bodoni) – 1999

Italian designer Antonio Pace created the font Linotype Gianotten™ in 2000. It is a new interpretation of the classic Bodoni font, for which Pace went back to Giambattista Bodoni's original punches, kept in a museum in Parma, and reinterpreted the 200-year-old characters for the world of modern digital technology. Rigorous design and the organic, unadorned construction of the individual characters give Linotype Gianotten™ a contemporary, highly readable appearance.

abcdefghijklm

nopqrstuvwxyz

1234567890

(. , - : ; ! ? ' ' * [& % §)

A B C D E F G H I

J K L M N O P Q R

S T U V W X Y Z

LTGianotten Regular

Gianotten – Antonio Pace (1970, Giambattista Bodoni) – 1999

abcdefghijklm
nopqrstuvwxyz

ABCDEFGHI
JKLMNOPQR
STUVWXYZ

1234567890

$%&(.,;:'"'"!?)@

Corporate identity for the city of
Milan by Antonio Pace, AREA
Strategic design. The adaptation
of a classic into a modern face.

Alfred Tilp, born in 1932, completed an apprenticeship in lithography before studying at the art academies of Stuttgart, Dusseldorf and Berlin. His major influence is Walter Brudi in Stuttgart. Tilp defines himself primarily as a typographer but is also active as a freelance artist and has recently been working on computer graphics (website: TilpArt.de).
He has been designing typefaces since 1967 and his work has been shown in numerous exhibitions and personal shows. Tilp has also written books on art and poetry and has had work published in such magazines as *Baseline*. From 1964 onwards, he taught, first at the Werkkunstschule Mainz, then at the Fachhochschule Rheinland-Pfalz and later at the Fachhochschule Würzburg. He became a professor in 1973 and retired in 1996. One of his fonts, Markin, is in the Linotype Library, and other fonts of his include Bardi (URW) and TilpSerif (Elsner-Flake). Markin is named after the writing utensil with which it appears to have been drawn, the marker pen. Its even strokes display characteristics similar to those of a sans-serif typeface, but the stroke endings, with their typical handwritten look, give Markin a personal touch. Extremely versatile, it is the perfect choice for any work where individuality and spontaneity are the emphasis.

abcdefghijklm

nopqrstuvwxyz

1234567890

(.,-:;!?''*[&%§)

A B C D E F G H I

J K L M N O P Q R

S T U V W X Y Z

Markin LT Regular

Elch fett 2.7.95

Work showing the creation process of
Markin. The original name, Elch, which
could not be used, was inspired by
a quote from the typeface designer
Paul Renner.

abcdefghikl

nnnoprstst

uuvw

AABBCDEFG

HKLMNPQ

RSTUVWXYZ

Markin – Alfred Tilp – 1999

Design suggestions by Manfred Baierl,
using Tilp's Markin LT, for the music
company Hoche-Musikverlag.

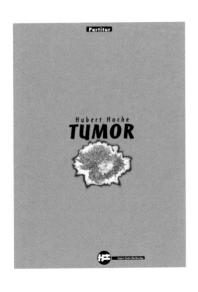

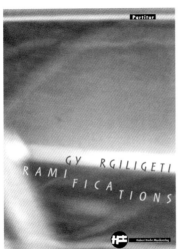

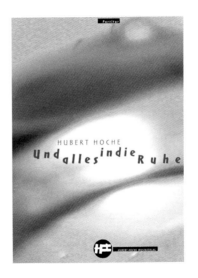

Scarborough - Akira Kobayashi - 1998

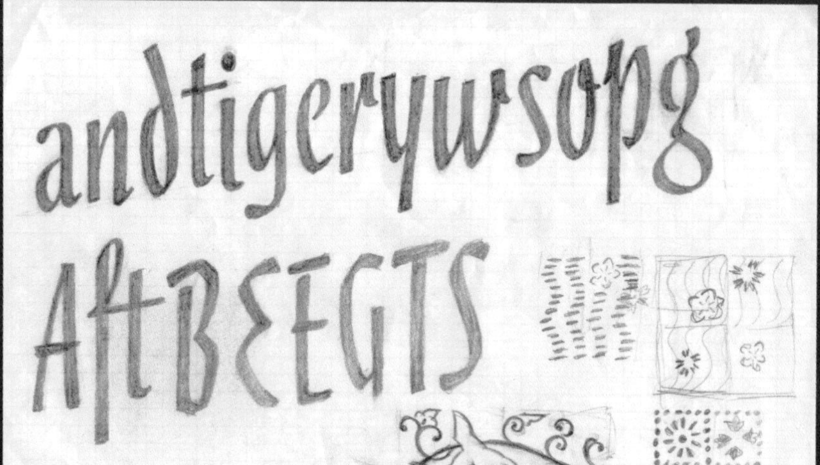

Akira Kobayashi studied at Musashino Art University in Tokyo and went on to complete a calligraphy course at London College of Printing. After finishing his studies, Kobayashi started work in the typeface design department of Sha-ken Co. Ltd, Japan. At the end of 1990, he moved to Jiyu-kobo Ltd, Japan and then to TypeBank Co. Ltd, Japan in 1993. In 1997, Kobayashi embarked on a freelance career as a type designer. From April 1998 to April 2001, he taught lettering at Nihon Designer Gakuin (polytechnic) in Tokyo and, from October 2000 to April 2001, he was part-time curator of the printing workshop at the Printing Museum in the same city. Since May 2001, Kobayashi has been type director of Linotype Library. He has received numerous awards, such as the titles 'Best of Category' and 'Best of Show' for the typeface Clifford in U&lc magazine's type design competition in 1998. In the Kyrillitsa 1999 competition, he won an award for ITC Japanese Garden and, in 2000, Conrad won him first prize in the text category of Linotype Library's 3rd International Digital Type Design Contest.

ITC Scarborough was designed in 1998 and is reminiscent of the typefaces in the advertisements of the 1930s. The special written form of the font has no connection between the letters and follows the principles of the brush scripts often used in the headlines and film trailers of that era. Kobayashi chose dynamic forms for the font: small yet robust, with contrast between the strokes. ITC Scarborough is available in regular and bold weights and is best used for headlines and short texts.

a b c d e f g h i j k l m

n o p q r s t u v w x y z

1 2 3 4 5 6 7 8 9 0

(. , - : ; ! ? ' ' * [& % §)

A B C D E F G H I

J K L M N O P Q R

S T U V W X Y Z

g % b

ITC Scarborough

ITC Scarborough™

Kobayashi has created a number of
poetic applications for his alphabet.

ITC SCARBOROUGH BOLD

JIVE PARTY

Soul Saturday!

Pennies from Heaven

Chicago Symphony Orchestra

Tchaikovsky's "Pathetique" 3rd Movement

ITC SCARBOROUGH REGULAR

SYMPHONIE

Acoustic Session

Fünf Orchesterkonzerte

The Immediate Singles Collection

Elgar's "Pomp and Circumstance" March No. 4

Silvermoon – Akira Kobayashi – 1998

Hamburgerfonts geß
Hamburgerfonts

ITC Silvermoon was designed in the style of advertisements from the 1920s. Art Deco was the main artistic movement in the years between the two world wars, combining elements of Jugendstil, Futurism and eastern Asian influences. ITC Silvermoon continues this tradition. The small, high-reaching figures, with their elegant forms and reserved but distinguishing loops, give the font its unmistakable look. It has two weights: regular and bold. To retain the elegance of the bold weight, the consistent stroke width of the regular weight was exchanged for contrasting strokes, giving the font more weight without detracting from its grace. The nostalgic, romantic ITC Silvermoon is best used for headlines and short texts in point sizes of 12 or higher and on less high-key illustrations and photos.

a b c d e f g h i j k l m

n o p q r s t u v w x y z

1 2 3 4 5 6 7 8 9 0

(. , - : ; | ? ' ' * [& % §)

A B C D E F G H I

J K L M N O P Q R

S T U V W X Y Z

mw

ITC Silvermoon Regular

ITC SILVERMOON BOLD

EMPIRE

Ornaments

TWENTIETH CENTURY

Leave no space undecorated

ITC SILVERMOON REGULAR

ADELPHI

Modernism

ARCHITECTS IN THE 30S

Le Corbusier's L'Esprit Nouveau

Silvermoon has highly decorative letters
full of romantic nostalgia for the 1920s.

Atomatic – Johannes Plass – 1997

doggy

German designer Johannes Plass created the fonts Linotype Animalia, Linotype Atomatic and Linotype Auferstehung in 1997. The fonts were selected for inclusion in the Take Type Library, following Linotype's International Digital Type Design contests in 1994 and 1997. Plass designed Linotype Atomatic in one strongly crafted weight and the font seems to reflect the fast pace and technology of modern times. The slight lean to the right gives an impression of speed and movement. Linotype Atomatic is intended exclusively for headlines in large point sizes.

abcdefghijklm

nopqrstuvwxyz

1 2 3 4 5 6 7 8 9 0

[. , - : ; ! ? " ` K [& º | o]

A B C D E F G H 1

J K L M N O P Q R

S T U V W X Y Z

LTAtomatic

MUTABOR ist das Forum für Kunst und Gestaltung an der Mathesisnochschule Kiel

Heinrich Paravicini founded the magazine *Mutabor* (Latin for *I am going to change*) at Mathesis University Kiel in 1993. Johannes Plass joined the *Mutabor* team in 1994. In 1998, they both decided to turn the design and magazine team into a design agency, also called Mutabor.

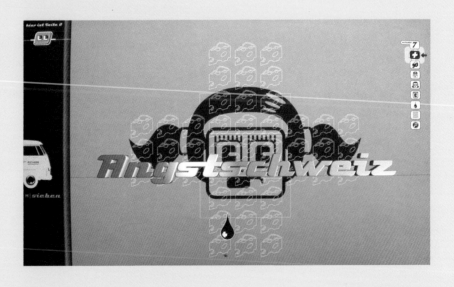

wasch dich frei!

Dabei hatte alles so gut angefangen. In dieser jungen Republik übernahmen Frauen nach dem Zusammenbruch des 3. Reiches alle Verantwortung. Sie bauten als „Trümmerfrauen" die Städte wieder auf, versorgten die Kinder und übernahmen die Geschäfte. Es wurde offen über die Frage nach der Verantwortlichkeit der Männer im 2. Weltkrieg gesprochen und geschrieben.

Die aus der Gefangenschaft zurückgekehrten Männer hatten nicht die Möglichkeit dem viel entgegenzusetzten. Zunächst überließen sie den Frauen das Handeln. Doch das sollte sich bald ändern. Der deutsche Mann erlangte sein Selbstbewußtsein zurück, und brachte sich wieder in die Gesellschaft ein. Arbeitsplätze waren rar zu Beginn der Fünfziger und sollten auf jeden Fall von einem Mann, dem traditionellen Ernährer der Familie, besetzt werden. Der Platz der Frau war wieder im Haus. Ihre Aufgabe war, für ein gemütliches Heim zu sorgen, das Essen zuzubereiten und sich vor allem um die Kinder zu kümmern. Diese Tradition unterstützte, wenn der Kindersegen reichlich ins Haus schneite, die neue CDU Regierung mit Prämien.

Aber auch die Werbung , früher Reklame und Propaganda, tat alles, um der Frau ihren Platz zuzuweisen. Sie zeigt jede Menge ganz natürlich lächelnde Frauen, mit denen man zwanglos für eigentlich alles wirbt. Am liebsten aber für die Körperpflege-, Kosmetik- und Waschmittelprodukte. So erfährt frau auch, daß mit Tampax das Jahr sieben Wochen mehr hat, ein Geheimnis, das mich noch heute erstaunt.

Die aktuellen Frauenzeitschriften wie „Frau und Film" oder „Constanze" setzten inhaltlich auf die fünf K's: Kinder, Küche, Kleider, Konsum und Komfort. Dort werden sogar Antworten auf 1000 Berufsfragen gegeben, doch gehen die Ratschläge eindeutig zurück zu den Frauenberufen wie Hundefriseurin oder Sekretärin.

Es gibt kleine Stifte zur Desodorierung. Diese aparte und aus Gründen des Taktes in ein Fremdwort verkleidete Bezeichnis bedeutet Geruch-Entfernung.

Chardonnay and Pinot Noir 2003 wine labels, designed by Jürgen Weltin.

Jürgen Weltin was born in 1969 in Constance, Germany. He worked in a publishing house before studying graphic design at the Technical College in Würzburg, during which time he went on an apprenticeship at the corporate design company Stankowski + Duschek and spent one term at Bournemouth & Poole College of Art and Design. The initial designs of the typeface Finnegan formed his graduation project at Würzburg under the guidance of Professor Reinhard Haus from Linotype Library. He went on to work as a graphic designer in an industrial firm where he was responsible for corporate design. In his spare time, he revised and extended the Finnegan typeface family. During the two years he spent at Stankowski + Duschek, he worked on new typefaces, including a new set of pictograms for the signage of the new Kunsthalle der Hypo-Kulturstiftung in Munich.

In September 1997, he joined Freda Sack and David Quay in their type foundry, The Foundry, in London, where he was involved in many development and production processes for such fonts as Foundry Gridnik and Foundry Form. In collaboration with Sack and Quay, who are valuable sources of inspiration and creative input, he designed many corporate typefaces (like the constructed alphabet for the new identity of the Odeon cinemas) and numerous logotypes for big international corporations. In 1999, Weltin was awarded a D&AD Silver Award for his typeface design for the Yellow Pages directory, which he started in February 1998 and finished in only three months, while still working at The Foundry. Jürgen Weltin lives and works in Stuttgart.

With his first typeface, Linotype Finnegan, Weltin endeavoured to create a modern sans-serif font with its roots in humanistic Old Face design. The harmonic proportions make it extremely legible. It is an extensive font family with 14 cuts, including both text and table numerals. Sans serifs are not usually used in long texts, as their neutrality and functionality quickly lead to fatigue and disinterest in the reader. The exciting challenge was to create a new sans-serif typeface that overcame these problems. The first sketches emerged in 1993, but were still too monoline. Many redrawings and proportional improvements ensued and, even at this early stage, the first figures were digitized to test the typeface's legibility.

The design was carried out almost entirely on screen with the help of Ikarus M. This process required enormous amounts of time but had a decisive advantage: with the help of print-outs, every single change could be immediately checked and corrected in different sizes. After about a year, a working font was ready. Then came further, massive changes in the stroke design and in the proportions of the single figures in relation to one another. At the same time, a semi-bold weight was designed, followed by an independent italic. Finally, Finnegan became a typeface family of four basic weights with corresponding italics and small caps. There is a recognizable direction of movement, based on writing, from upper left to lower right. The vertical strokes end in residual serifs, the thick strokes taper and the horizontal strokes and curves are noticeably thinner than the verticals. This dynamic design provides much liveliness and a high degree of variety by emphasizing contrasting directions.

Weltin's typeface Yellow was exclusive to British Telecommunications plc for the Yellow Pages directory. It also follows the internal structure of humanist Renaissance typefaces but is designed in a contemporary way for the special needs of a phone book. The typeface had to be extremely spatially economic, clear and highly readable at very small sizes and used with negative leading. To achieve this, Weltin created a sans serif distinguished by the simplicity of its design and condensed letterforms, with great height in the lowercase letters. Drawing the bold weight first gave him the opportunity to investigate the degree to which the letterforms could actually be condensed. Condensed letterforms tend to have a vertical appearance that is obstructive to reading speed, so the stroke design was given a slight calligraphic flow to emphasize the movement to the right and to help lead the eye along the line. To avoid inktraps caused by drawing deep cut-ins where vertical and horizontal strokes join (a method used for high-speed printing on low-quality, short-life paper), the horizontal strokes were treated in a radical and straight manner. The sharp movement of the horizontals away from the vertical stem created a lot more white space around the joining strokes. This treatment is essential to the function of the design and enables the symbols to be kept very open, enhancing a fortuitous combination of legibility and technical restraints.

abcdefghijklm

nopqrstuvwxyz

1234567890

(.,-:;!?''*[&%§)

¶&

A B C D E F G H I

J K L M N O P Q R

S T U V W X Y Z

LTFinnegan Medium

206

HIS SCUTSCHUM FESSED, with archers strung, helio, of the second. Hootch is for husbandman handling his hoe. Hohohoho, Mister Finn, you're going to be Mister Finnagain! Comeaday morm and, O, you're vine! Sendday's eve and, ah, you're vinegar! Hahahaha, Mister Funn, you're going to be fined again!

ROLLSRIGHTS, CARHACKS, stonengens, kisstuanes, tramtrees, fargobawlers, autokinotons, hippo-hobbilies, streetfleets, tournintaxes, megaphoggs, circuses and wardsmoats and basilikerks and aero-pagods and the hoyse and the jollybrool and the peeler in the coat and

a b c d e f g h ij k l m n ∼ o p q r s t u v w x y z ℰ

Finnegan Regular *& Italic*

WHAT THEN AGENTLIKE brought about that tra-goady thundersday this municipal sin business? Our cubehouse still rocks as earwitness to the thunder of his arafatas but we hear also through successive ages that shebby choruysh of unkalified muzzleni-miissilehims that would blackguardise the white-stone ever hurtleturtled out of heaven.

THE MECKLENBURK BITCH bite at his ear and the merlinburrow burrocks and his fore old porecourts, the bore the more, and his blightblack working-stacks at twelvepins a dozen and the noobibusses sleighing along Safetyfirst Street and the derry-jellybies snooping around Tell-No-Tailors' Corner and the fumes and

a b c d e f g h ij k l m n ∼ o p q r s t u v w x y z ℰ

Finnegan Medium *& Medium Italic*

STAY US WHEREFORE in our search for tighteous-ness, O Sustainer, what time we rise and when we take up to toothmick and before we lump down upown our leatherbed and in the night and at the fading of the stars! For a nod to the nabir is better than wink to the wabsanti.

THE HOPES AND THE strupithump of his ville's indigenous romekeepers, homesweepers, dome-creepers, thurum and thurum in fancymudmu-rumd and all the uproor from all the aufroofs, a roof for may and a reef for hugh butt under his bridge suits tony) wan warning

a b c d e f g h ij k l m n ∼ o p q r s t u v w x y z ℰ

Finnegan Bold *& Bold Italic*

OTHERWAYS WESWAYS LIKE that provost scoffing bedoueen the jebel and the jpysian sea. Cropherb the crunchbracken shall decide. Then we'll know if the feast is a flyday. She has a gift of seek on site and she allcasually ansars helpers, the dreamydeary. Heed! Heed!

PHILL FILT TIPPLING FULL. His howd feeled heavy, his hoddit did shake. (There was a wall of course in erection) Dimb! He stottered from the latter. Damb! he was dud. Dumb! Masta-batoom, mastabadtomm, when a mon merries his lute is all long. For the whole world to see.

a b c d e f g h ij k l m n ∼ o p q r s t u v w x y z ℰ

Finnegan Extra Bold *& Extra Bold Italic*

It may half been a missfired brick, as some say, or it mought have been due to a collupsus of his back promises, as others looked at it. (There extand by now one thousand and one stories, all told, of the same). But so sore did abe ite ivvy's holired abbles, (what with the wallhall's horrors of

Shize? I should shee! Macool, Macool, orra whyi deed ye diie? of a trying thirstay mournin? Sobs they sighdid at Fillagain's chrissormiss wake, all the hoolivans of the nation, prostrated in their consternation and their duodisimally profusive plethora of ululation.

Two letterproof pages with texts by
James Joyce, designed by Jürgen Weltin.

‹Now be aisy, good **Mr Finnimore**, sir.

[...] **Bygmester Finnegan, of the Stuttering Hand,**

riverrun, past Eve and

His scutschum fessed, with archers strung, helio, of the

And take your laysure like a god on

freemen's maurer, lived in the broadest way

Adam's, from swerve of

second. Hootch is for husbandman handling his hoe.

pension and don't be walking abroad.

immarginable in his rushlit toofarback for

shore to bend of bay,

Hohohoho, Mister Finn, you're going to be Mister Finnagain!

Sure you'd only lose yourself in

messuages before joshuan judges had given us

brings us by a commodius

Comeaday morm and, O, you're vine! Sendday's eve and, ah,

Healiopolis now the way your roads in

numbers or Helviticus committed deuteronomy

vicus of recirculation

you're vinegar! Hahahaha, Mister Funn, you're going to be

Kapelavaster are that winding there after

(one yeastyday he sternely struxk his tete in a tub

back to Howth Castle

fined again! What then agentlike brought about that tragoady

the cavalry, the North Umbrian and the

for to watsch the future [...]

and Environs.

thundersday this municipal sin business?

Fivs Barrow and Waddlings Raid.‹

abcdefghijklmnopqrstuvwxyzäöüß

ABCDEFGHIJK
LMNOPQRSTU
VWXYZÄÖÜ!?

SPITZ

Poster, 1997,
300 x 594mm.

Graphic designer Oliver Brentzel created Linotype Spitz™ in 1997. Brentzel comments, 'The motif of the Chrysler building in the poster symbolizes for me the language of form, which is also the basis for the Spitz font. A combination of pointed and semicircular elements develop their own aesthetic value through their interplay. Neither the Chrysler building nor Spitz is designed on the basis of geometric rules; they both take account of optical phenomena in their design.'

abcdefghijklm

nopqrstuvwxyz

1234567890

(.,-:;!?''‘*[&%§)

A B C D E F G H I

J K L M N O P Q R

S T U V W X Y Z

bwd

Poster, 1999, 215 x 610mm.
Poster, 1999, 215 x 610mm.

Cover of *Arena* supplement,
2001, 230 x 298mm.
Cover of *Arena* supplement,
2001, 230 x 298mm.

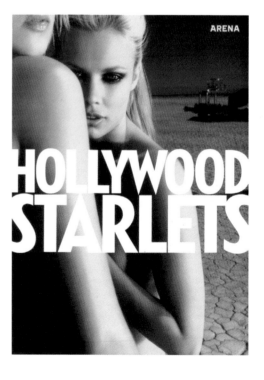

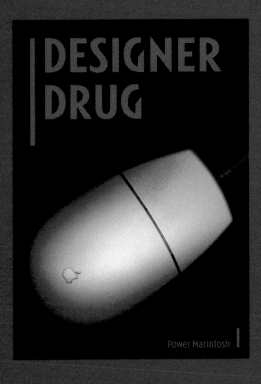

Poster, 1997, A1.
Poster, 1999, A2.

Poster, 1997, A1.
Poster, 1997, A1.

CARUMBA – JILL BELL – 1996

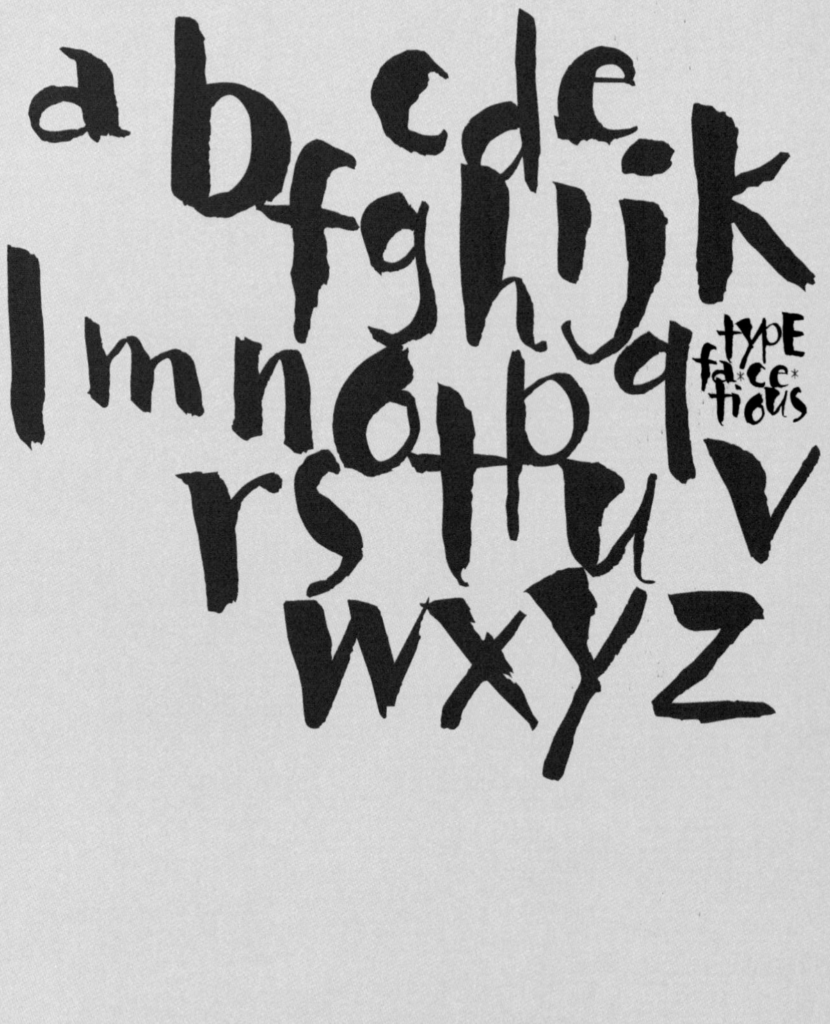

a b c d e
f g h i j k
l m n o p q
type
face-
tious
r s t u v
w x y z

Born in San Diego, California, Jill Bell now lives and works in Los Angeles creating logotypes, icons and handlettering for advertising, packaging and entertainment and producing web and print design. Bell has designed and digitized original faces for Fontek (Letraset), ITC, Adobe, Agfa/Monotype and Linotype, as well as for such clients as Disney and Johnson & Johnson. Most of her commercial lettering work captures and retains a handwritten feel and this is equally true of the majority of her fonts, such as Gigi and Smack. Bell is a graduate of UCLA and Otis/Parsons. She worked as a calligrapher, a sign painter and a production artist for Saul Bass before going into business by herself.

Bell's designs are informed by her broad knowledge of letter creation, from ancient inscriptions and writing to contemporary graffiti and tagging, and of diverse cultural traditions – she has studied devanagari, siddham and kanji. Her work is stylish, contemporary, fun and funky.

All her typefaces to date were formed initially by hand and created with a traditional broad-edged calligraphy pen, a pointed copperplate pen, a dry-bristle brush, a pointed Chinese brush, a Sharpie or even the wrong end of a brush (in the case of Smack) and then digitized and refined.

The Carumba font sizzles and snaps with hot Latin American exuberance and style. This exciting three-in-one design offers a spicy trio of initialling capitals, a complementary versatile lowercase and an abundance of alternative letters.

a b c d e f g h i j k l m

n o p q r s t u v w x y z

1 2 3 4 5 6 7 8 9 0

(. , - : ; ! ? ' ' * [& %)

A B C D E F G H I

J K L M N O P Q R

S T U V W X Y Z

carumba

type fa*ce*tious

Earth-
shattering
quotations.
featuring
the font
designs
of Jill
Bell

fa•ce•tious (fá-sē′ shés) *adj.*
Playfully jocular; humorous. —fa•ce′ tious•ly *adv.*
—face′ tious•ness *n.*

Rick Cusick | NYX Editions 2002

Typefa*ce*tious is Bell's typeface
sample book, designed by Rick
Cusich in 2002.
Bell's logos for Los Vatos and the
Cholo Girls were the inspiration
behind Carumba.

CARUMBA - JILL BELL - 1996

TOO MUCH OF A GOOD THING IS DE...

Carumba Hot Caps with Carumba Plain

A

BCDEFGH
IJKLMNO
PQRSTU
VWXYZ

V

ABCDE
FGHIJKL
MNOPQR
STUWXYZ

moce
{ abcdefghijklmn
opqrstuvwxyz }

nocey
abcdefghijk
lmnopqrstuvwxyz

noce
 abcdefghijklmn
opqrstuvwxyz

Zuzana Licko is co-founder of Emigre. Born in 1961 in Bratislava, Czechoslovakia, she emigrated to the USA in 1968. She graduated in graphic communications from U.C. Berkeley in 1984, the same year that Emigre magazine was founded. It garnered much critical acclaim when it began to incorporate Licko's digital typeface designs, created using the first generation of the Macintosh computer. The exposure of her typefaces in Emigre led to the production of Emigre Fonts, which Emigre now distributes worldwide. Typeface designs by Zuzana Licko include Modula (1985), Coarse Resolution (1985), Lo-Res (1985 and 2001), Citizen (1986), Matrix (1986), Lunatix (1988), Oblong (1988), Senator (1988), Variex (1988), Elektrix (1989), Triplex (1989), Triplex Greek (1989), Journal (1990), Modula Tall Greek (1990), Senator Tall Greek (1990), Tall Pack (1990), Totally Gothic & Totally Glyphic (1990), Matrix Script Greek (1992), Matrix Script (1992), Quartet (1992), Quartet Cyrillic (1992), Narly (1993), Dogma (1994), Whirligig (1994), Base Nine and Twelve (1995), Base Nine Cyrillic (1995), Modula Round & Ribbed (1995), Soda Script (1995), Filosofia (1996), Mrs Eaves (1996), Mrs Eaves Ligatures (1996), Base Monospace (1997), Hypnopaedia (1997), Tarzana (1998), Solex (2000) and Fairplex (2002).

Licko explains: 'Before the age of personal computers, when I used to spec typefaces out of phototypesetters' style books, my favourite typeface was Bodoni. I was attracted to its clean lines and geometric shapes and the variety of headline style choices. For practical reasons, however, I often decided against using Bodoni for long texts, as the extreme contrast made it difficult to read at small sizes. Since then, there have been many digital font revivals and reworkings of Bodoni's typefaces, some of which have brought to light the numerous variations in Bodoni's type designs not evident in the earlier photo types. The recent ITC Bodoni, for example, was released in three variants, each optimized for a range of sizes and each with very distinct features, reflecting the variety of Bodoni's work. Bodoni, in fact, spent his entire life building up a large collection of over 400 fonts. He started with Fournier's types as a model and, over time, developed a personal style that tended toward simplicity, austerity and a greater contrast between the vertical stems and hairlines than previously seen, resulting in what we know today as the modern face. In the preface of his Manuale Tipografico Bodoni stated, "It is proper here to present the four different headings from which it seems to me the beauties of type are derived. The first of these is regularity – conformity without ambiguity, variety without dissonance, and equality and symmetry without confusion."

This apparent development towards the geometry of Modern Face may explain the prevalence of excessively geometric Bodoni revivals, which may have gone a step further in this progression than Bodoni intended. Bodoni's many fonts also included small increments in sizes, sometimes down to half-point sizes. As was common practice at the time, each size varied in design to accommodate the effects of the printing process. The characters comprising small text sizes were slightly widened to accommodate ample counters, which resisted the tendency to clog up, as well as reducing contrast to ensure that the hairlines would not break up. The display sizes, in turn, were slightly narrower with more contrast, yielding graceful and delicate features, which the letterpress process could only maintain at the larger sizes. This practice disappeared with the introduction of phototype, as it became most efficient to simply scale a single design to the various sizes as needed. Since then, technical advancements, including improvements in the printing process itself, have made it less necessary to have size-specific design variations. It does, however, remain a necessity for the optimum legibility of certain designs, such as Bodoni, which were designed for different manufacturing and printing processes than those used today. In fact, the extreme contrast problem of many Bodoni revivals may be the result of choosing a display size for the model, which subsequently causes the hairlines to erode when reduced to small text sizes.

Although the computer is capable of addressing multiple size masters more readily than phototype did (for example, Adobe's Multiple Master format), optical scaling still needs to be added as a standard feature to the popular font formats, although it probably never will be, as most contemporary typefaces designed for today's technology do not make such critical demands of technical wizardry. As Bodoni created so many variations, many different Bodoni revivals and interpretations are possible. Which most truly reflect Bodoni's work, however, can be eternally debated.

Filosofia is my interpretation of a Bodoni. It shows my personal preference for a geometric Bodoni, while incorporating such features as the slightly bulging round serif endings, which often appeared in printed samples of Bodoni's work and reflect Bodoni's origins in letterpress technology. The Filosofia Regular family is designed for text applications. It is somewhat rugged, with reduced contrast to withstand the reduction to text sizes. The Filosofia Grand family is intended for display applications and is therefore more delicate and refined. An additional variant, included in the Grand package, is a Unicase version, which uses a single height for characters that are otherwise separated into upper- and lower-case. This is similar to Bradbury Thompson's Alphabet Twenty Six, except that Thompson's goal was to create a text alphabet free of such redundancies as the two different forms that represent the character "a" or "A", whereas Filosofia Unicase does have stylistic variants to provide flexibility for headline use. My research for Filosofia included studying various versions of Bodoni, from Bodoni's original print work to recent revivals such as ITC Bodoni. I did not, however, use any particular specimen as the model. Rather, I drew my Bodoni from memory, akin to the process of transcribing, while following the guideline of rough measurements to retain the basic proportions. I followed the same process for Mrs Eaves, my Baskerville revival. There are many details in my revivals without an historical origin, such as the rounded terminals of the lowercase 's' in Filosofia, which was a design decision within the context of the rounded serifs I chose. When drawing a revival, I question the form of each character and element according to my own sensibilities, as though I were drawing it as an original design.'

abcdefghijklm

nopqrstuvwxyz

1 2 3 4 5 6 7 8 9 0

(. , - : ; ! ? ’ ‘ * [& % §)

ABCDEFGHI

JKLMNOPQR

STUVWXYZ

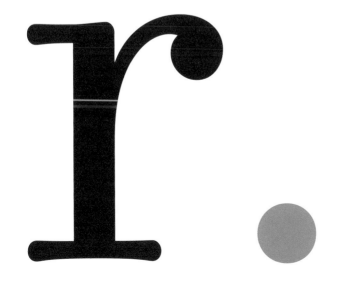

Filosofia Regular

Filosofia — Zuzana Licko — 1996

Applications for Filosofia, based on
Bodoni, by Zuzana Licko, *Emigre*
magazine, no. 42, 1997.

Filosofia

Filosofia Regular
7/7 point

Typi non habent claritatem insitam; est usus legentis in iis qui facit eorum claritatem. Investigationes demonstraverunt lectores legere melius quod ii legunt saepius. Claritas est etiam processus dynamicus, qui sequitur mutationem consuetudinum lectorum. Mirum est notare quam littera gothica, quam nunc putamus parum claram, anteposuerit litterarum formas humanitatis per saecula quarta decima et quinta decima. Eodem modo typi, qui nunc nobis videntur parum clari, fiant sollemnes in futurum.

Filosofia Italic
7/7 point

Typi non habent claritatem insitam; est usus legentis in iis qui facit eorum claritatem. Investigationes demonstraverunt lectores legere melius quod ii legunt saepius. Claritas est etiam processus dynamicus, qui sequitur mutationem consuetudinum lectorum. Mirum est notare quam littera gothica, quam nunc putamus parum claram, anteposuerit litterarum formas humanitatis per saecula quarta decima et quinta decima. Eodem modo typi, qui nunc nobis videntur parum clari, fiant sollemnes in futurum.

Filosofia Bold
7/7 point

Typi non habent claritatem insitam; est usus legentis in iis qui facit eorum claritatem. Investigationes demonstraverunt lectores legere melius quod ii legunt saepius. Claritas est etiam processus dynamicus, qui sequitur mutationem consuetudinum lectorum. Mirum est notare quam littera gothica, quam nunc putamus parum claram, anteposuerit litterarum formas humanitatis per saecula quarta decima et quinta decima. Eodem modo typi, qui nunc nobis videntur parum clari, fiant sollemnes in futurum.

Filosofia Regular
10/10 point

Typi non habent claritatem insitam; est usus legentis in iis qui facit eorum claritatem. Investigationes demonstraverunt lectores legere melius quod ii legunt saepius. Claritas est etiam processus dynamicus, qui sequitur mutationem consuetudinum lectorum. Mirum est notare quam littera gothica, quam nunc putamus parum claram, anteposuerit litterarum formas humanitatis per saecula quarta decima et quinta decima. Eodem modo typi, qui nunc nobis videntur parum clari, fiant sollemnes in futurum.

Filosofia Italic
10/10 point

Typi non habent claritatem insitam; est usus legentis in iis qui facit eorum claritatem. Investigationes demonstraverunt lectores legere melius quod ii legunt saepius. Claritas est etiam processus dynamicus, qui sequitur mutationem consuetudinum lectorum. Mirum est notare quam littera gothica, quam nunc putamus parum claram, anteposuerit litterarum formas humanitatis per saecula quarta decima et quinta decima. Eodem modo typi, qui nunc nobis videntur parum clari, fiant sollemnes in futurum. Typi non habent claritatem insitam; est usus legentis in iis qui facit eorum

Filosofia Bold
10/10 point

Typi non habent claritatem insitam; est usus legentis in iis qui facit eorum claritatem. Investigationes demonstraverunt lectores legere melius quod ii legunt saepius. Claritas est etiam processus dynamicus, qui sequitur mutationem consuetudinum lectorum. Mirum est notare quam littera gothica, quam nunc putamus parum claram, anteposuerit litterarum formas humanitatis per saecula quarta decima et quinta decima. Eodem modo typi, qui nunc nobis videntur parum clari, fiant sollemnes

Filosofia Regular
Filosofia Italic
Filosofia Bold

&

FILOSOFIA
SMALL CAPS

&

FRACTIONS

Designed by Zuzana Licko

Based on Bodoni

FIVE FONTS: FILOSOFIA REGULAR, FILOSOFIA ITALIC, FILOSOFIA BOLD, FILOSOFIA SMALL CAPS & FRACTIONS: $95.00
ORDER BY PHONE: (800) 944 9021 - ORDER ON-LINE: WWW.EMIGRE.COM - ORDER BY FAX: (916) 451 4351

ALL ORNAMENTS FROM FILOSOFIA FRACTIONS FONT.

H

Filosofia Grand

Filosofia Grand Bold

FILOSOFIA
GRAND CAPS

All ornaments from Filosofia Fractions font.

FILOSOFIA UNICASE

Four Fonts: Filosofia Grand, Filosofia Grand Bold, Filosofia Grand Caps & Filosofia Unicase: $95.00
Order by phone: (800) 944 9021 · Order on-line: www.emigre.com · Order by fax: (916) 451 4351

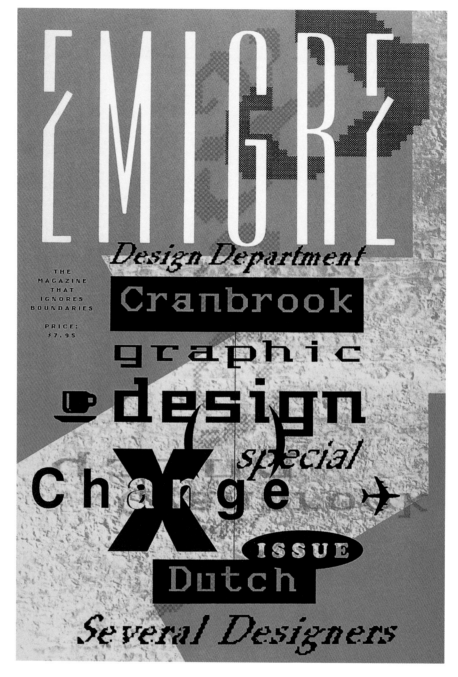

EMIGRE

Design Department

THE
MAGAZINE
THAT
IGNORES
BOUNDARIES

PRICE:
$7.95

Cranbrook

graphic

design

special

Change

ISSUE

Dutch

Several Designers

Rudy VanderLans is also co-founder
of Emigre. He studied at the Royal
Academy of Art in The Hague and, after
working in the Netherlands for several
years, moved to California, where he
studied photography at U.C. Berkeley.
In 1984, VanderLans set up *Emigre*
magazine, a journal for experimental
graphic design, with his wife
Zuzana Licko.

Typeface designs by Rudy VanderLans
include Oblong (1988), Variex (1988)
and Suburban (1993).

Cover by Rudy VanderLans and Zuzana
Licko. Pages 2–3 and 32–inside back
cover. Glenn A. Suokko and Emigre
Graphics, *Emigre*, 1988.

This exchange between Cranbrook designers and Dutch designers manifests itself
here in a variety of forms, attitudes and
philosophies. The exchange becomes a
comparison as it exists here in print, docu-
menting time, place, the individual and
cultural identity.

We would like to thank all of the participants, Esther Vermeer, Helene Bergmans
and Vincent van Baar of Studio Dumbar, Rick Vermeulen and Laura Grevinger of
Hans Winsor, Harry Arnett of Pisces, Rene DeHaan of Ancotone, Lisa Anderson,
Andrew Maxwell, Arch Garland, Allen Hori, Darcee Kessel, Susan Lally, Tamar
Rosenthal, Scott Santoro, and Scott Zukowski of Cranbrook Academy of Art Design
Department, Vincent van Baar, Eric van Casteren, Bart de Groot, Gerard van
Leyden, Max Kisman, Tosh Mulder, Ron van Roon, and Michel van der Sanden
from The Netherlands and Edward Fella, Jeffrey Keedy, Ed MacDonald, William
Summers, Lucille Tenazas and Rudy Van der Lans from the United States for their
responses to the post cards, and Jan Jancourt and Ed MacDonald, Cranbrook
Academy of Art graduates who participated in internships in The Netherlands. Kath-
erine McCoy, CoChairman, Cranbrook Academy of Art Design Department, for her
guidance and support, and a special thank you to Roov Van der Lans for his
interest and confidence in our work and for allowing us the opportunity to
develop this issue of Emigre.

This issue

of Emigre Magazine is devoted to the exchange and transfer of culture
expressed visually and verbally by Cranbrook Academy of Art design students and
several Dutch designers. The project began when Emigre publisher, Rudy Van
der Lans, asked us to conceptualize and design an issue of Emigre Magazine
focusing our attention on graphic design and the exchange between the
Cranbrook Academy of Art Design Department and several Dutch design groups
including Studio Dumbar, Dirt Haag, and Hans Winsor, Rotterdam. Individual
Dutch designers from Philips Corporate Industrial Design, Eindhoven, Total Design,
Amsterdam and Vorm Vijf, Amsterdam, also contributed to the project. The
following are individual proposals and design solutions which all deal with
cultural and cross-cultural stereotypes, experiences, and expectations. Each
Cranbrook Design student proposed a design problem to individual Dutch
designers. The proposals were directed toward individual interpretation and/
or expressions of the designer's particular culture. Cranbrook Design students
responded to their own proposals as well. The ongoing exchange that takes place between Cranbrook design students.

Dutch design studios and Dutch visiting artists has been an enriching and inspir-
ing experience for everyone involved. Among Dutch visiting artists to Cranbrook
are Gert Dumbar, Studio Dumbar; Rick Vermeulen, Hard Werken; Professor R. D. Oxenaar
of the PTT; and Anton Beeke. Design students from Cranbrook Academy of Art
participate yearly in internships with Studio Dumbar and most recently with Philips,
Total Design and Vorm Vijf. The exchange exceeds beyond graphic design, as many
lasting friendships and professional relationships have developed over the
years. More importantly, it has been the cultural exchange that has had the most
profound effect on each individual. In understanding culture we must compare
cultures. In describing our own cultures, we learn about other cultures. In
discussing the differences or similarities between cultures, we define our own
culture.

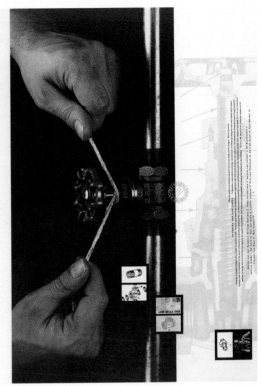

culture THE NETHERLANDS

several Dutch designers

TRAN

CODE BLEU

CODE
BLEU

Rudy VanderLans, Zuzana Licko and
Emigre Graphics, *Emigre*, 1993.
Cover Rudy VanderLans and Zuzana
Licko. Pages 72–73 and 94–95.

a_liat_LL. – AL_ssio ' .ona, .i – 1996

&

Good Type needs good Cheese

BuyMyFonts.com

Italian designer Alessio Leonardi has created the fonts F2F Al Retto™ (1996), F2F Allineato™ (1995), F2F CoolWool™ (1994), HaManga Irregular™ (1994), F2F Madame Butterfly™ (1996), F2F Mekanik Amente™ (1993), F2F Mekkaso Tomanik™ (1994), F2F Metamorfosi™ (1995), F2F Poison Flowers™ (1994), F2F Prototipa Multipla™ (1996), F2F Provinciali™ (1995), F2F Tagliatelle Sugo™ (1996), F2F Ale™ (1994) and F2F Simbolico™ (1994).

The techno sound of the 1990s, a personal computer, font-creation software and some innovation were the sources of the F2F (Face2Face) font series. Leonardi and his friends were commissioned to create new, unusual faces for the leading German techno magazine Frontpage. Even typeset in 6 points, to the degree of virtual illegibility, it was a pleasure for kids to read and decipher the articles.

abcdefghijklm

nopqrstuvwxyz

1234567890

(.,-:;!?'"*[&%§)

ABCDEFGHI

JKLMNOPQR

STUVWXYZ

Sst!

F2FTagliatelle-Sugo

Pages from the German techno
magazine *Frontpage*, designed by
Alessio Leonardi in 1996.

fun adventures

Alle Records
Alle Parties
Alle Dates
Alle Tricks

AWeX
EmmanuelTop
JimiTenor

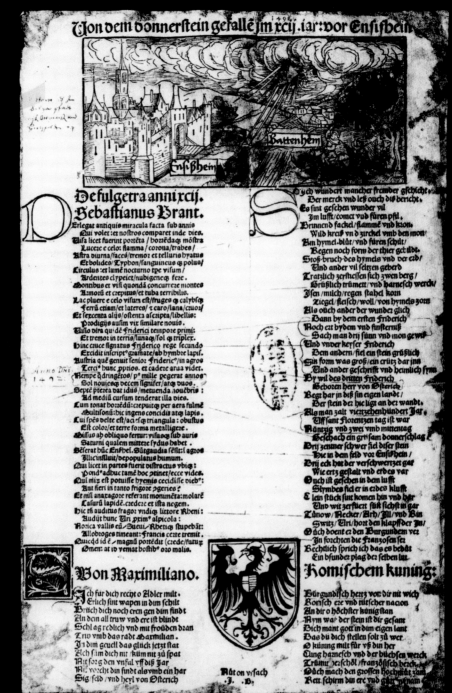

New techniques, new letters, new typography. The first really new newspaper letter was Morris Fuller Benton's Century in 1900, which he was commissioned to design by *Century* magazine. In England, such new fonts as Ionic and Clarendon followed, and Ionic was the model for the revised Texttype published in 1929 in the USA. After that came Excelsior and then in 1932 came Times New Roman, designed by Stanley Morison for the London paper *The Times*. Times was drawn from examples of Old Style, a Renaissance Antiqua letter. In the 1960s, now-familiar faces, such as Concorde, Swift and Edison, were created. In the 1990s, with new technological developments and the advent of the digital era, there was a clear need for a new newspaper typeface with optimal legibility. The brief for Linotype's designers was that the various characters should generate a totally new face with its own individual personality. The new LinoLetter alphabet had to be clearly recognizable, with quality, legibility and technical processing playing a major role. The overall design had to be harmoniously defined by the proportion, the weight and the ratios between the capitals, the x-height and the serifs. The result was a comfortably readable, closed font, introduced in 1992.

The first news publications were in the form of pamphlets. Here, an example from 1492 is set in Rotunda, a round Gothic script.

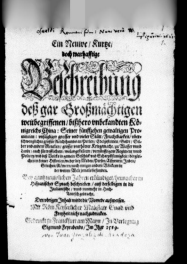

A message from the Kingdom of China, published in Frankfurt in 1589. Printed in red and black.

The first monthly newspaper, *Annus Christi*, was published in Rorschag aan de Bodensee, Switzerland in 1597.

A description of the history of Michael von Aitzing, 1588. A predecessor of the first periodical, this was published biannually in Frankfurt.

In 1620, 14 different weekly newspapers were published in Germany, all of which were highly influential. *Relation*, shown here, was first published in 1609 in Strasbourg.

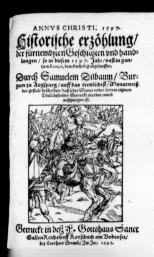

Classic fonts from the headlines of European daily newspapers. *Gazzetta di Genova* is set in Bodoni-Antiqua, the fonts for *Le Moniteur Universel* and *Le Fédéral* are versions of Didot, while *The Times* and *The Daily News* are variants of William Miller's font from 1813.

abcdefghijklm

nopqrstuvwxyz

1 2 3 4 5 6 7 8 9 0

(. , - : ; ! ? ' ' * [& % §)

ABCDEFGHI

JKLMNOPQR

STUVWXYZ

pqrs

LinoLetter LT Roman

H n

b h

m

LinoLetter promotes legibility and
rapid comprehension.

C G

a c

f r

2 3

Didot – Linotype (1784, Firmin Didot) – 1991

Didot, the rediscovery of classicism;
a sensitive, contemporary revision of
Didot Antiqua. The model was an
historic publication from 1819,
La Henriade, set in the original Didot.
The origin of Didot Antiqua goes back
over a period of more than a hundred
years to the family of the same name.
These Antiqua letters were significant not
only for classicism but also for European
typography, and Firmin Didot, 1764–1836,
occupies a special place in the history of
typography and type design.

By the second half of the 20th century,
Antiqua had fallen entirely into oblivion,
but with the development of photosetting,
offset printing and, later, the digital era,
it was again possible to breathe life into
this fragile Didot font. A letter with a
marked contrast between the strong
verticals and the fine serifs, Didot also
has beautiful neo-classical elements that
embellish and support the text.

abcdefghijklm

nopqrstuvwxyz

1234567890

(. , - : ; ! ? ' ' * [& % §)

A B C D E F G H I

J K L M N O P Q R

S T U V W X Y Z

p q

Didot LT Roman

DIDOT 1991

Didot Antiqua

Firmin Didot

1784

CHANT CINQUIÈME.

CEPENDANT s'avançaient ces machines mortelles
Qui portaient dans leur sein la perte des rebelles :
Et le fer, et le feu, volant de toutes parts,
De cent bouches d'airain foudroyaient leurs remparts.
Les Seize et leur courroux, Mayenne et sa prudence,
D'un peuple mutiné la farouche insolence,
Des docteurs de la loi les scandaleux discours,
Contre le grand Henri n'étaient qu'un vain secours :
La victoire, à grands pas, s'approchait sur ses traces.
Sixte, Philippe, Rome, éclataient en menaces :
Mais Rome n'était plus terrible à l'univers ;
Ses foudres impuissants se perdaient dans les airs ;
Et du vieux Castillan la lenteur ordinaire
Privait les assiégés d'un secours nécessaire.
Ses soldats, dans la France errant de tous côtés,

VARIANTES.

CHANT PREMIER.

Vers 1 et suiv.; 1re édition, Londres, 1723, in-8°,

Je chante les combats et ce roi généreux
Qui força les Français à devenir heureux,
Qui dissipa la ligue et fit trembler l'Ibère,
Qui fut de ses sujets le vainqueur et le père,
Dans Paris subjugué fit adorer ses lois,
Et fut l'amour du monde et l'exemple des rois.
  Muse, raconte-moi quelle haine obstinée
Arma contre Henri la France mutinée;
Et comment nos aïeux, à leur perte courants,
Au plus juste des rois préféraient des tyrans.

On dit qu'un Grec nommé Dadiky, qui se trouvait à Londres, vit par hasard la première feuille de ce poëme, et que, choqué du second vers, il alla trouver l'auteur, et lui dit : Monsieur, je suis du pays d'Homère; il ne commençait pas ses poëmes par un trait d'esprit, par une énigme.

L'édition de 1723 fut faite par l'abbé Desfontaines sur un manuscrit informe dont il s'était emparé : il en fit une autre à Évreux qui est extrêmement rare, et dans laquelle il inséra des vers de sa façon.

Vers 59 et suiv.; édition de 1723,

Troublant tout dans Paris, et, du haut de ses tours,
De Rome et de l'Espagne appelant les secours;
De l'autre paraissaient les soutiens de la France,
Divisés par leur secte, unis par la vengeance :
Henri de leurs desseins était l'ame et l'appui;
Leurs cœurs impatients volaient tous après lui.
On eût dit que l'armée, à son pouvoir soumise,
Ne connaissait qu'un chef et n'avait qu'une église.

fexab.
sgozj

BORN IN ZURICH IN 1961, MARCO GANZ ATTENDED THE ZURICH SCHOOL OF DESIGN, AFTER WHICH HE COMPLETED A GRAPHIC-DESIGN APPRENTICESHIP. IN 1983, HE ESTABLISHED HIS OWN GRAPHIC-DESIGN STUDIO, WORKING IN NEW YORK FROM 1987 TO 1989 AND THEN RETURNING TO ZURICH. GANZ'S DESIGNS INCLUDE LINOTYPE MANO, A SCRIPT-LIKE TEXT FACE, AND LINOTYPE VETO SANS-SERIF TYPE FAMILY. HE WON SWISS NATIONAL DESIGN PRIZES IN 1990 AND 1996 AND HAS BEEN AN INDEPENDENT ARTIST SINCE 1993, REPRESENTED BY GALERIE BRIGITTE WEISS, ZURICH, SINCE 1998. VETO WAS THE RESULT OF A DESIRE TO DESIGN AN INNOVATIVE SANS-SERIF FACE. STARTING WITH SINGLE LETTERFORMS, GANZ OMITTED EVERYTHING HE CONSIDERED OLD-FASHIONED OR SUPERFLUOUS, SEEKING NEW SOLUTIONS AND IGNORING OLD RULES WHEREVER NECESSARY. VETO'S LOWERCASE LETTERS, FOR EXAMPLE, ARE NORMAL-WIDTH CHARACTERS, WHILE THE UPPERCASE LETTERS ARE DRAWN IN PERCEPTIBLY DIFFERENT, MUCH NARROWER PROPORTIONS. THIS CONCEPT REFLECTS GANZ'S VIEW THAT OVERLY NARROW LOWERCASE LETTERS (SUCH AS ROTIS) ARE POORLY LEGIBLE AND THAT UNDULY WIDE CAPITAL LETTERS NOT ONLY LOOK OUTMODED BUT ALSO TAKE UP TOO MUCH SPACE (AS IN HELVETICA). GANZ ADMITS TO BEING INSPIRED BY FRUTIGER, ROTIS AND GERSTNER ORIGINAL FACES. HE DID NOT FOLLOW ANY OBVIOUS TRENDS, RATHER HE CONTRADICTED THEM, SO THE TYPE FAMILY HAS ONLY 8 WEIGHTS, THE TRULY NECESSARY ONES. IT ALSO LACKS THE CURRENTLY FASHIONABLE OLD-STYLE FIGURES, SMALL CAPS AND A DECORATIVE, CALLIGRAPHIC ITALIC, WHICH GANZ THOUGHT OUT OF DATE AND THEREFORE UNNECESSARY IN A MODERN SANS-SERIF FAMILY. VETO WAS DRAWN BY HAND, AND WHILE GANZ'S FORMAL EXPERIMENTS AT THE OUTSET PRODUCED UNUSABLE CHARACTERS, IT WAS PRECISELY THOSE DISCARDED FORMS AND ENDLESS REVISIONS THAT ULTIMATELY RESULTED IN THE MANY INNOVATIVE SOLUTIONS THAT DEFINE VETO'S UNIQUE PERSONALITY. GANZ SEES VETO AS A CONTEMPORARY ALTERNATIVE TO THE MOST POPULAR SANS SERIFS THAT HAVE PERHAPS BEEN USED JUST A BIT TOO OFTEN. VETO IS VERY VERSATILE BUT IS PARTICULARLY GOOD FOR MAKING A TYPOGRAPHIC STATEMENT, FOR INSTANCE, IN A COMPANY'S CORPORATE IDENTITY. THE ITALIC VERSIONS ARE SUITED TO A DYNAMIC APPROACH.

abcdefghijklm

nopqrstuvwxyz

1234567890

(.,-:;!?''*[&%§)

A B C D E F G H I

J K L M N O P Q R

S T U V W X Y Z

348&

LTVeto Medium

Keke **ROSBERG** *:* Williams FW08 Cosworth
Nelson **PIQUET** *:* Brabham BT52/BT52B BMW
Alan **JONES** *:* Williams FW07/FW07b Cosworth
Jody **SCHECKTER** *:* Ferrari 312T4
Mario **ANDRETTI** *:* Lotus 78 Cosworth
Niki **LAUDA** *:* Ferrari 312T2
James **HUNT** *:* McLaren M23 Cosworth
Niki **LAUDA** *:* Ferrari 312T
Emerson **FITTIPALDI** *:* McLaren M23 Cosworth
Jackie **STEWART** *:* Tyrrell 006 Cosworth
Emerson **FITTIPALDI** *:* Lotus 72 Cosworth
Jackie **STEWART** *:* Tyrrell 003 Cosworth
Jochen **RINDT** *:* Lotus 72 Cosworth
Jackie **STEWART** *:* Matra MS10 Cosworth
Graham **HILL** *:* Lotus 49 Cosworth

A typeface without flourishes, Veto is
modest and communicative. Marco Ganz
is a typographer and plastic artist.
Shown here are four simple, clear
sculptures for the typeface.

Karlgeorg Hoefer was born in 1914 in Schlesisch-Drehnow, Germany. Following his schooling in Schlesien and Hamburg, he served a four-year typesetting apprenticeship in Hamburg (1930–34). After two years of military service, he studied at the Kunstgewerbeschule (School of Arts and Crafts) in Offenbach am Main and went on to work in Potsdam. From 1939 to 1945, he was in active military service, which included a spell as a prisoner of war in Russia.

Hoefer's activities as a calligrapher began after working as a calligraphy teacher at the Werkkunstschule in Offenbach. He developed a universal pen with novel writing and drawing techniques for the Brause company, and, as result of this, he began to design typefaces, the first of which was Salto™, published by the Brothers Klingspor. In quick succession, Hoefer created numerous typefaces, including Saltino, Saltarello and Monsun (1954), Prima (1957), Stereo (1968) and Bigband™ (1974), to name a few. Some of his more recent typefaces are Omnia™ and San Marco™ (1990), and Sho™ Roman and Notre Dame™ (1991), which were already conceived for use on the PC.

From 1970 to 1979, Hoefer was a lecturer and then a professor at the HfG (School of Design) in Offenbach. In 1976, he lectured at the Institute for Fine Arts in Cluj, Romania. From 1981 to 1988, he ran summer calligraphy workshops in the USA (Los Angeles, San Francisco, Boston, New York, Washington and other cities). In 1982, he founded an open-entry calligraphy workshop in Offenbach, with evening courses and a summer school, and, in 1987, he set up the registered association 'Calligraphy Workshop Klingspor, Offenbach, Supporters of International Calligraphy'.

From 1987 to 1995, he was chairman of the association, while continuing to teach courses and summer school classes with leading foreign calligraphers. Hoefer has written two books on calligraphy: Das alles mit einer Feder (All That With a Feather) (Brause, 1953) and Kalligraphie, gestaltete Handschrift (Calligraphy, Designed Handwriting) (Econ, 1986). Numerous articles on Hoefer's work have appeared in calligraphy journals in Holland, France, the USA and Japan. In 1989, the book Schriftkunst/Letterart Karlgeorg Hoefer (The Letter Art of Karlgeorg Hoefer) was published by Calligraphy-Editions Herbert Maring. Outstanding one-man exhibitions were held in 1963 and 1984 at the Klingspor Museum in Offenbach and, in 1966, a travelling exhibition took place in Scandinavia. Hoefer also exhibited at the Gutenberg-Museum in Mainz (1975), in San Francisco (1982), in Berkeley, California (1983), in New York (1990), at the Chamber of Industry and Commerce in Offenbach and Bad Soden (1994) and at the Archive of the Klingspor Calligraphy Workshop (1996). Karlgeorg Hoefer's innovation in calligraphy is also reflected in the variety of materials he used in his work.

For his activities as a calligrapher, Hoefer received the Silver Citizens Medal from the City of Offenbach in 1989 and was distinguished with the Order of Merit of the Federal Republic of Germany in 1993. He died on 8 October 2000 in Offenbach. Sho first appeared in 1992, published by Linotype-Hell. The face is recognizable by the extreme contrast between strokes and the way it uses simple, round forms in some of its letters, giving it a peppy and playful feel. The name Sho comes from the Japanese and reflects the Japanese art of writing.

abcdefghijklm

nopqrstuvwxyz

1 2 3 4 5 6 7 8 9 0

(. , - : ; ! ? ' ' * [& % §)

A B C D E F G H I

J K L M N O P Q R

S T U V W X Y Z

Sho LT Roman

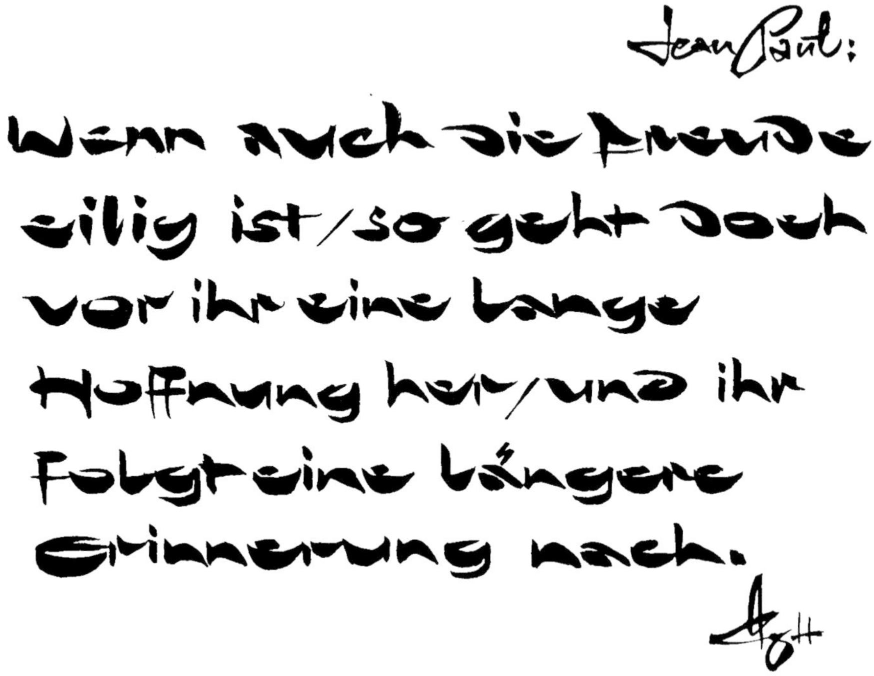

Jean Paul:

Wenn auch die Freude
eilig ist/so geht doch
vor ihr eine lange
Hoffnung her/und ihr
folgt eine längere
Erinnerung nach.

der pinsel tanzt
pinsel
die tusche singt
tanzt

OLYPUS

Born in The Hague, the Netherlands in 1961, Peter Matthias Noordzij is a typographer, type designer and teacher. He studied at the Royal Academy of Fine Arts in The Hague from 1980 to 1985, attending lectures in lettering taken by his father, Gerrit Noordzij. In 1983, during his third year of study, he produced preliminary sketches for his PMN Caecilia™ typeface. In 1985 and 1986, he underwent practical training in a printing works, going on to work as a typographer in 1986.

Clients have included the publishers Querido, Arbeiderspers and Meulenhoff and the daily newspaper de Volkskrant. From 1986 to 1989, Noordzij taught typography in Arnhem and, from 1988 onwards, type design at the art academy in The Hague. Since 1991, he has been in charge of the new Enschedé Font Foundry in Haarlem.

PMN Caecilia™ was released in 1991. This slab-serif font distinguishes itself in the completeness of each cut, which comes with small caps and Old Style figures, such details giving designers finer control over their own creations.

abcdefghijklm

nopqrstuvwxyz

1234567890

(.,-:;!?'ʼ*[&%§)

ABCDEFGHI

JKLMNOPQR

STUVWXYZ

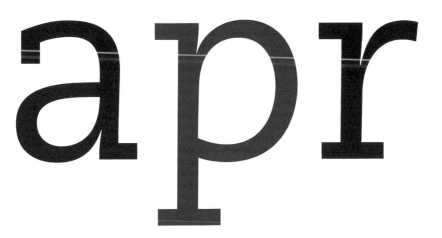

apr

Caecilia LT Roman

PMN Caecilia – Peter Matthias Noordzij – 1990

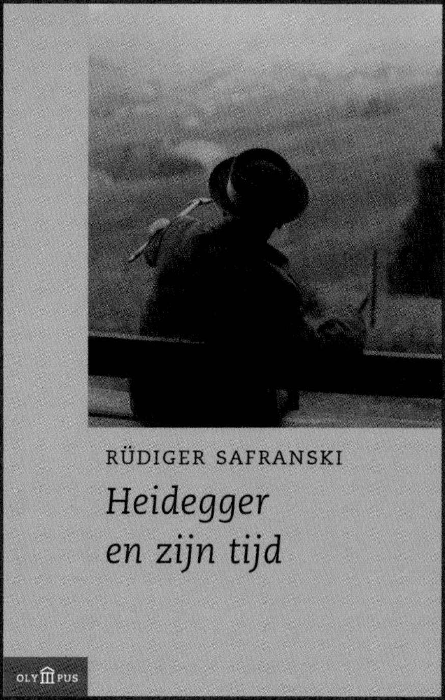
RÜDIGER SAFRANSKI
Heidegger
en zijn tijd

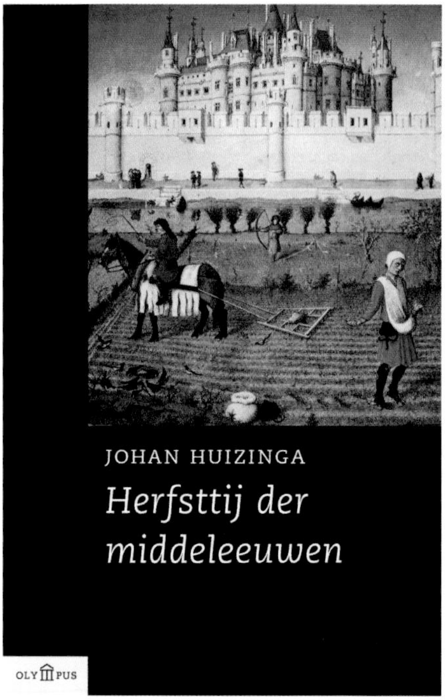
JOHAN HUIZINGA
Herfsttij der
middeleeuwen

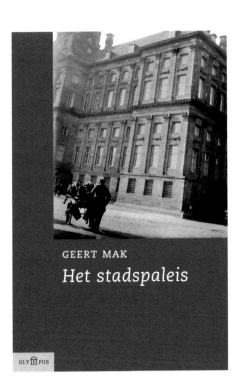

Four book covers for the publishing house Olympus, designed by Geert de Koning using Caecilia.

GEERT MAK
Het stadspaleis

OLY ⅢPUS

DAVID QUAMMEN
Het lied
van de dodo

OLY ⅢPUS

© erik spiekermann | 99

		BOOK	O
			O
			O
			O
		MEDIUM	O
			O
			O
		BOLD	O
			O
			O
		EXTRABOLD	O
			O
			O
			O
		BLACK	O
			O
			O
			O

af	SANS
af	SERIF
af	SANS ITALIC
af	SERIF ITALIC
AF	SANS CAPS
AF	SERIF CAPS
AF	SANS ITALIC CAPS
AF	SERIF ITALIC CAPS
13	LINING FIGURES
13	OLD STYLE FIGURES

«A typeface with a
ffi-ligature in its name
can't be *all* bad»

ED CLEARY,
COOPER & BEATTY

ITC **Officina**

ITC Officina

Officina combines the honest "information only" look of a typewriter face with the benefits of better legibility, additional stylistic choices, & more economical use of space.

ITC Officina is available in two families: sans and serif; each in five weights of roman, *italic*, SMALL CAPS with both lining and old style figures. *ITC Officina was designed by Erik Spiekermann in 1989.* Digital help for the book & bold versions came from Just van Rossum. *The medium, extrabold & black weights as well as all the small caps were digitized by Ole Schäfer in 1998.*

Traits like the left-pointing serif of the i and j, the tail of the lowercase l, and the slightly heavy punctuation, which link this design to its typewriter-like cousins, also serve the dual purpose of improving character legibility.

ITC Officina was originally conceived as a typeface to bridge the gap between old fashioned typewriter type and a traditional text face. It has since become *the* cool face in new media.

Officina is a narrow face, quite economical. Counters are full and serifs sufficiently strong to withstand the rigors of small sizes, telefaxing, less than ideal paper stock & modest screen resolutions.

Erik Spiekermann, born 1947, refers to himself as a typographic designer and a type designer. He financed his studies in art history at Berlin's Free University by running a printing press and setting metal type in the basement of his house. After spending seven years as a freelance designer in London, he returned to Berlin in 1979, where – together with two partners – he founded MetaDesign. The company specializes in complex – often large – corporate design programmes and information systems, including new media, online and offline, all with strong emphasis on typography. In 1989, Spiekermann founded FontShop International, the publishers of the FontFont library. One of his own designs, FF Meta, is published by the library and has become one of the most popular typefaces in the USA and Europe. ITC Officina, another of his typefaces, seems to be on every other web page these days and FF Info, his latest effort, has been chosen for the navigation system in a major European airport.

Spiekermann started designing type back in the 1970s by redrawing such old hot-metal faces from the Berthold library as LoType and Berliner Grotesque. He has written numerous articles and four books on type and typography, including Stop Stealing Sheep *for Adobe Press, which have appeared both in Europe and the USA. He is on the board of directors of the ATypI, a member of the Type Directors Club New York, an honorary member of the Typographic Circle London, a fellow of the International Society of Typographic Designers UK, vice-president of the German Design Council and president of the International Institute for Information Design. He holds an honorary professorship at the Academy of Arts in Bremen and teaches workshops at design schools around the world. His entertaining lectures and often controversial participation in competition juries have gained him international repute as one of Germany's leading communication designers. Spiekermann's work, and that of MetaDesign, has been credited as offering a blend of teutonic efficiency and Anglo Saxon humour. In August 2000, Spiekermann left MetaDesign Berlin due to policy disagreements. He now works as a freelance design consultant in Berlin, London and San Francisco.*

Officina embodies the ideals of efficient office communication in its serif and sans-serif forms, both of which are designed and spaced to offer optimal legibility. Its style is that found on a traditional typewriter, altered to suit modern technological developments.

a b c d e f g h i j k l m

n o p q r s t u v w x y z

1 2 3 4 5 6 7 8 9 0

(. , - : ; ! ? ′′ * [& % §)

A B C D E F G H I

J K L M N O P Q R

S T U V W X Y Z

WXV

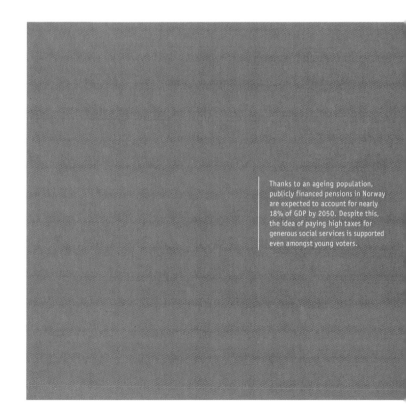

Thanks to an ageing population, publicly financed pensions in Norway are expected to account for nearly 18% of GDP by 2050. Despite this, the idea of paying high taxes for generous social services is supported even amongst young voters.

ITC Officina

ITC Officina was originally conceived as a typeface to bridge the gap between old fashioned typewriter type and a traditional typographic design. The design goal was to create a small family of type ideally suited to the tasks of office correspondence and business documentation.

Midway through the design, however, it became obvious that this face had capabilities far beyond its original intention. Production tests showed that ITC Officina could stand on its own as a highly legible and remarkably functional type style.

The European design team, under the close guidance of the Berlin designer, Erik Spiekermann, was given the directive to continue the work on ITC Officina, but now with two goals. The first was to maintain the original objective of the design: to create a practical and utilitarian tool for the office environment. And the second was to develop a family of type suitable to a wide range of typographic applications.

What developed is a different sort of type family. It has a distilled range of just two weights: Book and Bold (medium weight being unnecessary in office correspondence) with complementary italics. In addition, ITC Officina is available in two styles: Serif and Sans. The end result is an exceptionally versatile communication tool packaged in a relatively small type family.

Proportionally, the design has been kept somewhat condensed to make the family space economical. Special care was also taken to insure that counters were full and serifs sufficiently strong to withstand the rigors of small sizes, modest resolution output devices, telefaxing, and less than ideal paper stock.

h h h h

The italic design could have been rendered as simple oblique romans, but cursive overtones were incorporated to provide distinction and character.

ITC Officina is available as a serif or sans serif design, in Book and Bold weights with corresponding italics.

Alternate numbers have been drawn to provide additional flexibility of use.

Traits like the left-pointing serif of the "i" and "j," the tail of the lowercase "l," and the slightly heavy punctuation, which link this design to its typewriter-like cousins, also serve the dual purpose of improving character legibility.

279

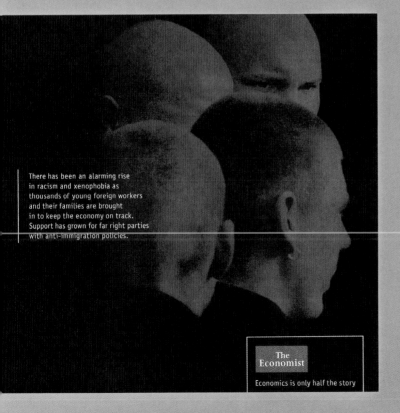

There has been an alarming rise in racism and xenophobia as thousands of young foreign workers and their families are brought in to keep the economy on track. Support has grown for far right parties with anti-immigration policies.

The Economist

Economics is only half the story

Three applications of Officina.

Industria/Insignia – Neville Brody – 1989

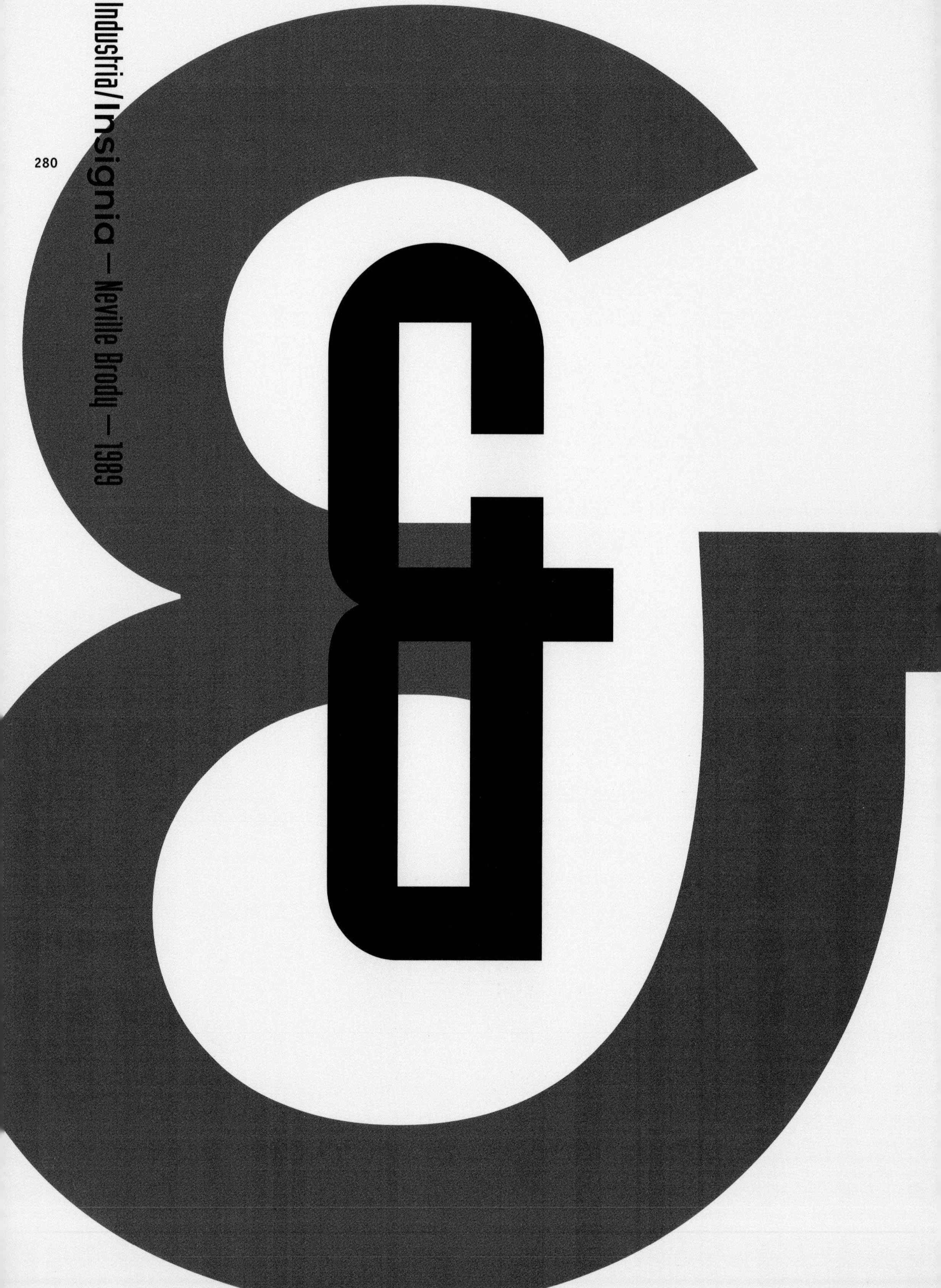

Neville Brody was born in 1957 in London. He is a graphic designer, art director and type designer, having studied painting at Hornsey College in 1975 and attending London College of Printing from 1976 to 1979. Brody has designed numerous record covers. From 1981 to 1986, he was art director of the UK magazine <u>The Face</u>. Between 1983 and 1987, he designed covers for the London magazine <u>City Limits</u> and, from 1987 to 1990, worked for the magazine <u>Arena</u>. He has acted as art director for the magazines <u>Per Lui</u> and <u>Lei</u> published by Condé Nast Publications in Milan and the French magazine <u>Actuel</u>. In 1988, Brody worked and designed for Nike, Premiere TV, ORF, the House of World Culture in Berlin, the Deutsches Theater in Hamburg, Parco department store in Tokyo and the digital medium of the publication <u>Fuse</u>. Brody's typographic style uses aesthetic elements from Art Deco and betrays non-European influences. His graphic language has become an international model for the new age of computer-oriented design. An exhibition of his work, 'The Graphic Language of Neville Brody', travelled between London, Edinburgh, Berlin, Hamburg, Frankfurt am Main and Tokyo from 1988 to 1990. Fonts by Brody include Arcadia™ (1990), Industria™ (1989), Insignia™ (1989), Blur (1991), Pop (1991), Gothic (1991) and Harlem (1991).

Industria™ was originally designed for <u>The Face</u> and released as a font by Linotype Library in 1989. Industria is a condensed sans serif with abbreviated, essential forms. It has a systemized mechanical structure of straight strokes with rounded outer corners and rectangular counter-spaces. The solid version is strong, cool and reserved; the inline version gives a vibrating and artful contrast. The alternate font has a more flamboyant lowercase 'g' and 't'.

Insignia™ was designed as a headline face for <u>Arena</u> in 1986 and released as a font by Linotype Library in 1989. It has the basic forms of constructed Grotesque fonts and was influenced by the New Typography of the Bauhaus during the 1930s. Its monoline, round-and-sharp forms reflect the Zeitgeist of that era, suggesting technology and progress, yet, like other Brody fonts, Insignia is also immediately recognizable as one of the trendy, cutting-edge classics of our own computer era. The alternate font has half serifs on the 'E', 'F', and 'Z', squeezed bowls on the 'P' and 'R', a wider 'J' and an 'S' made from protractor-shaped parts.

a b c d e f g h i j k l m

n o p q r s t u v w x y z

1 2 3 4 5 6 7 8 9 0

[. , - : ; ! ? ' ' * [& %]

A B C D E F G H I

J K L M N O P Q R

S T U V W X Y Z

P

abcdefghijklm

nopqrstuvwxyz

1234567890

(. , - : ; ! ? ' ' * [& % §)

A B C D E F G H I

J K L M N O P Q R

S T U V W X Y Z

Insignia LT

AUTU 30 £5.95

ARENA

WHAT'S IT ABOUT, ALFIE?

my name is michael caine exclusive interview by tony parsons

bedtime story fiction by raymond carver

body count despatches from the war zone; by john sweeney

trouser snake! sir les patterson's wardrobe

the bachelor pad/alexandra pigg/jean-michel basquiat
dean stockwell/maria cornejo/museums/the beer belly
thinking man's crumpet/travel writing/haoui montaug

36 pages of fashion: white shirts/man in
a suitcase/accessories/the colour of money

SIXTIES CAINE PHOTOGRAPHED BY DAVID BAILEY

A12

0 74470 72697 5

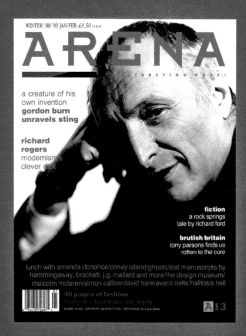

Brody's work is influenced by the New
Typography of the Bauhaus movement.

Industrial/Insignia – Neville Brody – 1989

CD cover for <u>Dance Wicked</u>,
released by the Quattro label.
Design by Neville Brody and
Nana Shiomi, 1990.

Adrian Frutiger Right from the beginning, I was convinced that Avenir is the better Futura. *Akira Kobayashi I share your opinion, but some weights have been missing to make Avenir an all-purpose typeface.* You mean the Condensed weights? *Yes, with this extension I'm sure Avenir will then be able to cut its own path.* Then we should get to work putting Avenir onto that path ... *Yes.*

The beautiful stranger, or why there is now an Avenir Next.

Adrian Frutiger has created such famous typefaces as Univers and Frutiger, but another issue has remained very close to his heart: the design of his linear sans serif, Avenir. In 1988, the Swiss font designer first presented Avenir, which at that time offered an excellent alternative to such other well-known typefaces as Futura and Avant Garde. Compared to the rather metrical construction of other faces, Avenir was drawn more humanely and more classically. It was originally released in 6 weights, which in typographic practice, proved to be a restricting factor, as did the missing bold weights. To realize Avenir's true potential as a contemporary typeface, this had to be rectified. With his love of linear symbols, Frutiger completely revised the Avenir font family in 2004, in close cooperation with Akira Kobayashi. The result was Avenir Next, with its harmoniously incremented weights and matching condensed versions, totalling 24 weights, including true small caps and Old Style figures. Avenir Next is a fully fledged contemporary Grotesque with a great degree of typographic flexibility.

abcdefghijklm

nopqrstuvwxyz

1234567890

(.,-:;!?''′*[&%§)

A B C D E F G H I

J K L M N O P Q R

S T U V W X Y Z

Q G

Avenir LT 55 Roman

✖✖✖ Gemeente Amsterdam

✖✖✖ Gemeente Amsterdam
Bestuursdienst

✖✖✖ Gemeente Amsterdam
Raadsgriffie

✖✖✖ Gemeente Amsterdam
Dienst Ruimtelijke Ordening

✖✖✖ Gemeente Amsterdam
Dienst Wonen

✖✖✖ Gemeente Amsterdam
ProjectManagement Bureau

✖✖✖ Gemeente Amsterdam
Ontwikkelingsbedrijf

✖✖✖ Gemeente Amsterdam
Afval Energie Bedrijf

✖✖✖ Gemeente Amsterdam
Waterleidingbedrijf

✖✖✖ Gemeente Amsterdam
Stadsdeel Osdorp

Gemeente Amsterdam

Avenir is a sans serif based on the principles of the New Objectivity of the 1930s. There are hints that the typeface was meant to be an interpretation of Futura, but, unlike Futura, Avenir is not purely geometric. The harmony of the forms was more important to Frutiger than exact geometry, and the typeface has a strong and sensible appearance. Its six weights complement each other perfectly and make it possible to set texts with nuanced grey tones.

Avenir is eminently suitable for complex design solutions. It offers a wide range of individual application options, while still ensuring a unified overall appearance. The City of Amsterdam was the first metropolis to fully adopt Avenir, thereby winning the coveted Dutch Corporate Identity Prize in 2003.

Frutiger Next – Adrian Frutiger – 2001

2001
Frutiger
Next

In the days of metal, Frutiger first experienced the power of type to make the whole intellectual world readable. This awakened in him the urge to develop the best possible legibility. The time soon came when texts were no longer set in metal types but by means of a beam of light, and the task of adapting the typefaces of the old masters from relief type to flat film was Frutiger's forte. When it came to the Grotesque style of sans serif, however, he had his own ideas, which led to the Univers™ family. Frutiger explains, 'From all these experiences the most important thing I learned was that legibility and beauty stand close together and that type design, in its restraint, should be only felt but not perceived by the reader.' In 1968, Frutiger was commissioned to develop a signage and directional system for the new Charles de Gaulle Airport in Paris. He decided to create a new sans-serif typeface suitable for the specific legibility requirements of airport signage: easy recognition from various distances and angles, whether driving or walking. The resulting font corresponded with the modern architecture of the airport.

In 1976, he expanded and completed the family for D. Stempel AG in conjunction with Linotype Library, and it was named Frutiger. The Frutiger™ family is neither strictly geometric nor humanistic in construction; its forms are designed so that each individual character is quickly and easily recognized. Such distinctness makes it good for signage and display work. Although it was originally intended for the large scale of an airport, the full family has a warmth and subtlety that has, in recent years, made it popular for the smaller scale body text in magazines and booklets.

Frutiger™ Next is Linotype Library's new interpretation of Frutiger, designed in conjunction with Adrian Frutiger and released in 2001. The goal was to create a complete system of 18 weights, placing priority on retaining the aesthetic aspects of the original characters while optically adjusting the contrast between weights. The italics in the original Frutiger were based very closely on the roman forms but have been re-designed in the new Frutiger Next to be true italics.

abcdefghijklm

nopqrstuvwxyz

1 2 3 4 5 6 7 8 9 0

(. , - : ; ! ? ' ' * [& % §)

A B C D E F G H I

J K L M N O P Q R

S T U V W X Y Z

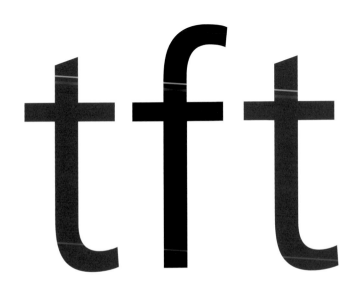

Frutiger Next LT Regular

The signage system for Charles
de Gaulle airport, 1972.

The Frutiger typeface is used
on this signage system for the
Swiss PTT and the French
motorways, 1972.

Les premières applications du caractère « Frutiger » par les PTT Suisse et les autoroutes françaises

Les bureaux de poste
des PTT Suisse
(conception Kurt Wälti)

Sur les autobus des PTT

L'animation touristique
des autoroutes
(conception Jean Widmer)

Le «Frutiger» adapté pour les textes imprimés

L'aspect de chaque caractère d'imprimerie est une chose complexe, où forme, mo uvement rhytme, et donc aussi les propo rtions, le réglage des approches, etc., ne se laissent plus dissocier. Dans tous les ra pports formels et autres relations il s'agit de phénomènes optiques irréductibles aux règles mathématiques et que seule pourra percevoir et fixer la sensibilité visuelle, qu'il s'agisse des détails de chaque série du même caractère, ou de la graduation distin guant réciproquement les diverses séries

L'aspect de chaque caractère d'imprimer ie est une chose complexe, où forme, mo uvement rhytme, et donc aussi les propo rtions, le réglage des approches, etc., ne se laissent plus dissocier. Dans tous les ra pports formels et autres relations il s'agit de phénomènes optiques irréductibles aux règles mathématiques et que seule pourra percevoir et fixer la sensibilité vis uelle, qu'il s'agisse des détails de chaque série du même caractère, ou de la gradua tion distinguant réciproquement les div

L'aspect de chaque caractère d'imprimer ie est une chose complexe, où forme, mo uvement rhytme, et donc aussi les propo rtions, le réglage des approches, etc., ne se laissent plus dissocier. Dans tous les ra pports formels et autres relations il s'agit de phénomènes optiques irréductibles aux règles mathématiques et que seule pourra percevoir et fixer la sensibilité vis uelle, qu'il s'agisse des détails de chaque série du même caractère, ou de la gradua tion distinguant réciproquement les div

Frutiger 56

302

1E.

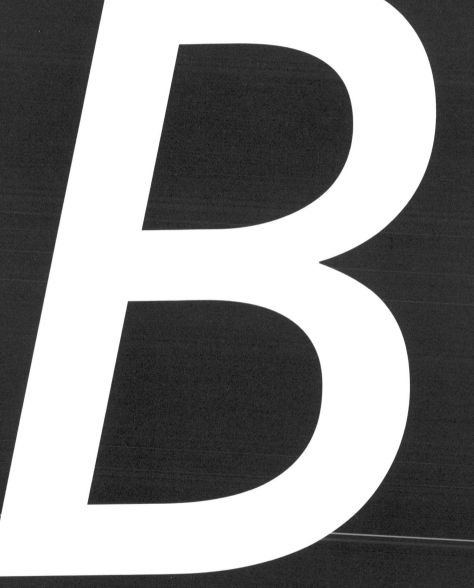

Frutiger's drawing of the letter 'B'
for Frutiger 56, Swiss Foundation,
Type and Typography.

Frutiger 56

32^r 32^r

Frutiger's drawing of the letter 'H'
for Frutiger 56, Swiss Foundation,
Type and Typography.

Stone – Summner Stone – 1987

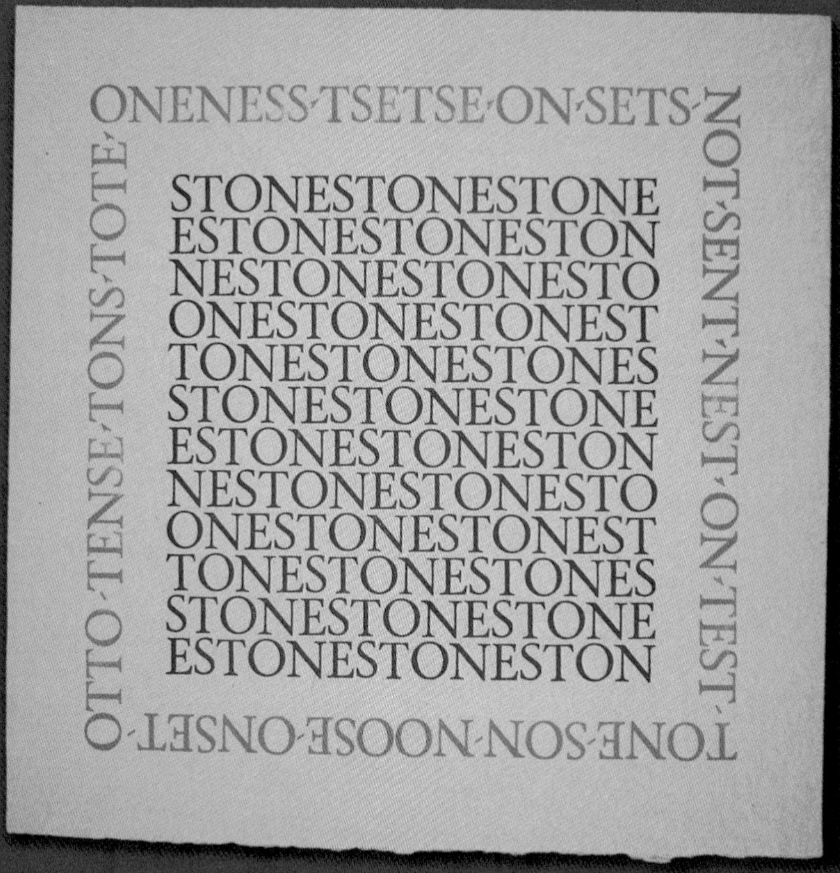

Born in 1945 in Venice, Florida, USA, Sumner Stone is a type designer and designer. In 1966, he studied at Reed College in Portland, Oregon, where he was taught calligraphy by Lloyd Reynolds. He went on to work as a type designer for Hallmark Cards in Kansas City for two years, and then, in 1972, he opened his type studio, Alpha and Omega Press, in Sonoma, California. At the same time, he was studying mathematics at Sonoma State University. In 1979, he accepted a position at Autologic Inc. in Boston as director of typography. He later held the same position at Camex Inc. in Boston and, from 1985 to 1989, at Adobe Systems Inc. in California. Adobe's first original fonts were Stone's Stone family typefaces, cut in a total of 18 weights. Working with Bob Ishi of Adobe, Stone created this family, which appeared in 1987. Coincidentally, *ishi* is the Japanese word for stone, which precluded any squabbling about whose name the font would carry. The family consists of three types of fonts: a serif, a sans serif and an informal style. The Stone face is very legible and makes a modern, dynamic impression.

In 1990, Stone opened his Stone Type Foundry for digital type design in Palo Alto, California, and, in 1991, he designed Stone Print for the American graphic-design magazine *Print*.

Fonts include Stone® Family (1987), Stone Print (1991), Stone Phonetic (with John Renner, 1992), Silica (1993), Bodoni™ Ornaments (1994), Bodoni™ Six (1994), Bodoni™ Twelve (1994) and Bodoni™ Seventy Two (1994–95).

abcdefghijklm

nopqrstuvwxyz

1234567890

(.,-:;!?''*[&%§)

A B C D E F G H I

J K L M N O P Q R

S T U V W X Y Z

P R

StoneSans LT

Stone – Sumner Stone – 1987

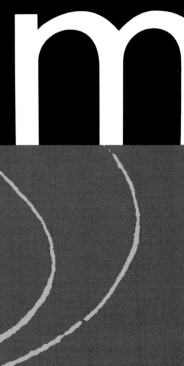

THE WORDS ON THE
PRINTED PAGE ARE
TO BE LOOKED AT
NOT LISTENED TO

El Lissitzky

In typographic design, craft deals with
points, lines, planes, picas, ciceros,
leads quads, serifs, letters words, pages
signatures, paper, ink, color, printing, and binding.

The vocabulary
of form (art)
includes, among
others:

Good design,
good typography,
Swiss or otherwise,
is a fusion of informa-
tion and inspiration,
of the conscious
and the unconscious
of yesterday
and today,
of fact and
phantasy,
work and play,
craft and art.

space
proportion
scale, site, shape,
rhythm, repetition,
sequence, movement,
balance, volume,
contrast,
harmony order,
and simplicity.

Paul Rand

313

Lucida – Kris Holmes/Charles Bigelow – 1985

Lucida

Kris Holmes was born in 1950 in Reedly, California, and works as a type designer. He studied from 1968 to 1971 at Reed College in Portland, Oregon, where he was taught calligraphy by Lloyd Reynolds and Robert Paladino. In 1975, he attended the Martha Graham School and the Alwin Nikolai School in New York (modern dance). He studied at the School of Visual Arts in New York in 1976, where he was taught lettering by Ephram E. Benguiatm, and at the Rochester Institute of Technology in Rochester, New York in 1979, where he was taught calligraphy and type design by Hermann Zapf. Holmes's calligraphic and lettering work has been printed in numerous magazines. In 1976, he and Charles Bigelow founded the company Bigelow & Holmes.

Holmes has designed over 75 fonts, including Leviathan (1979), Shannon (with Janice Prescott, 1982), Baskerville® (Revival, 1982), Caslon (Revival, 1982), ITC Isadora™ (1983), Sierra™ (1983), Lucida® (with Charles Bigelow, 1985), Galileo (1987), Apple New York (1991), Apple Monaco (1991), Apple Chancery (1994) and Kolibri (1994).

Lucida is a family of fonts with one basic design but offered in two variations. It has both serif and sans-serif characters and is suitable for books and text, documentation and business reports, posters, advertisements and multimedia.

abcdefghijklm

nopqrstuvwxyz

1234567890

(.,-:;!?'' * [&%§)

ABCDEFGHI

JKLMNOPQR

STUVWXYZ

LucidaSans Roman

one basic
design

two variat
ions

serif and
sans serif

design

basic one

ions

two variat

sans serif

serif and

The 1000 Lire banknote on which
Hermann Zapf first sketched the
letterforms that he would later use in
his design for Optima, Florence, 1950.

Optima™ was designed by Hermann Zapf and is his most successful typeface. In 1950, Zapf made his first sketches when visiting the Santa Croce church in Florence. He sketched letters from gravestones (cut around 1530) on two 1,000 lire bank notes as he had no other paper with him. These letters, from the floor of the church, were the inspiration behind Optima, a typeface that is classically roman in proportion and character, but without serifs. The letterforms were designed to the proportions of the Golden Ratio. After careful legibility testing, the first drawings were finished in 1952, and the type was cut by the famous punch cutter August Rosenberger at the D. Stempel AG type foundry in Frankfurt. Optima was produced in matrices for the Linotype typesetting machines and released in 1958. With the clear, simple elegance of its sans-serif forms and the warmly human touches of its tapering stems, the family has proved popular around the world. Available in 12 weights and 4 companion fonts with Central European characters and accents, it is an all-purpose typeface, working for just about anything from book text to signage. In 2002, more than 50 years after the first sketches, Hermann Zapf and Akira Kobayashi completed Optima™ nova, an expansion and re-design of the Optima family.

abcdefghijklm

nopqrstuvwxyz

1234567890

(. , - : ; ! ? ' ' * [& % §)

A B C D E F G H I

J K L M N O P Q R

S T U V W X Y Z

Optima nova LT Regular

Optima nova – Hermann Zapf – 2002

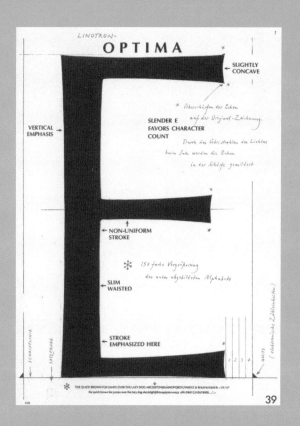

ABCDEFGHIJKLM
NOPQRSTUVWXYZ

·0123456789/

&AACHCODCEFTHE

HRKALALILLMENN

OOODQQURAReSA

STTTETHTITTUVÆ

ÄÆŒŎOØÜUÜÜ

€$¢£¥

The 'E' explains the principles behind Optima.

The Vietnam Veterans Memorial in Washington uses Optima for the more than 58,000 names of soldiers lost in the war.

The complete Optima alphabet with titling by Hermann Zapf.

Modern Classics: Fonts and Type Designers

Akzidenz Grotesk, 1969
Günter Gerhard Lange

Helvetica, 1957
Max Miedinger

Futura, 1932
Paul Renner

GillSans, 1928–30
Eric Gill

Times New Roman, 1832
Stanley Morison

Bodoni, 1790
Giambattista Bodoni

Baskerville, 1754
John Baskerville

Caslon, 1725
William Caslon

Stempel Garamond, 1543
Claude Garamond

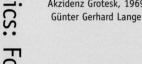

Akzidenz Grotesk, 1969
Günter Gerhard Lange

Helvetica, 1957
Max Miedinger

Futura, 1932
Paul Renner

GillSans, 1928–30
Eric Gill

Times New Roman, 1832
Stanley Morison

Bodoni, 1790
Giambattista Bodoni

Baskerville, 1754
John Baskerville

Caslon, 1725
William Caslon

Stempel Garamond, 1543
Claude Garamond

Soutien du Temple de mémoire,
Nous transmettons les Faits à la postérité;
Les Arts, les Sciences, l'Histoire
Nous doivent l'Immortalité.

MANUEL TYPOGRAPHIQUE,

UTILE

AUX GENS DE LETTRES,

& à ceux qui exercent les dif-
férentes parties de l'Art
de l'Imprimerie.

Par FOURNIER, le jeune.

TOME II.

A PARIS,

Chez l'Auteur, rue des Postes.
J. BARBOU, rue des Mathurins.

M. DCC. LXVI.

Akzidenz Grotesk – Günter Gerhard Lange – 1969

AkziD enzGr oTesK

Very simple and highly typical, 'AG', as connoisseurs like to call this typeface, was already more than twenty years old at the heyday of Constructivism. Followers of De Stijl, Bauhaus, Dada and others used AG to great effect. It was present at the birth of Swiss typography and became its major typeface. AG still has a high visual quality, proving that type does not have to be uniform to make it legible and attractive; on the contrary, it is the difference between characters that makes them legible. Two companies presented Akzidenz Grotesk in January 1899 in an advertisement in the German book and lithographic press; one was Berthold, the other Bauer & Co. in Stuttgart.

In 1973, Günter Gerhard Lange, AG's re-designer and type director of Berthold, described AG as follows: 'In this work, the basic proportions of the well-loved Akzidenz Grotesk semi-bold were used to determine the average length and individual shapes. The family similarities between the individual styles had of course to be taken into account, as did the mood of the times and fashion.' The fashion at that time was the brand new Helvetica by Max Miedinger and other new faces like Univers by Adrian Frutiger and Folio by Bauer. Still, good old AG continues to play a major role in the ever-changing world of printing and design.

abcdefghijklm

nopqrstuvwxyz

1234567890

(.,-:;!?'ʼ*[&%§)

A B C D E F G H I

J K L M N O P Q R

S T U V W X Y Z

AG

Akzidenz Grotesk

'Typefaces must be functional. The one you
are reading has been my favourite for 60
years. Its name is Akzidenz-Grotesk.'
Anton Stankowski, Stuttgart, 1989.

Akzidenz Grotesk – Günter Gerhard Lange – 1969

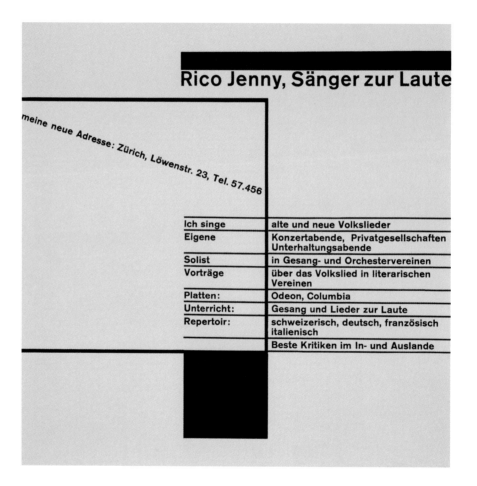

This 1930's advert by Stankowski is an
integrated design, which has lost none
of its freshness and originality even
after so many years.

Like many other old fonts, AG has never
fallen from grace. This is an advert for
AG from Berthold in the 1960s.

82631 6/6 p Min. ca 2 kg 120 a 84 A □□□ Sign. 85
Industrielle Formgebung ist nicht das Problem unserer Zeit.
Wenn Formen entstanden sind, und Formen entstehen, die mit
unserem heutigen Weltbild besser übereinstimmen als jene,
ZEITGEMÄSSE FORMGEBUNG DER HERSTELLUNGS-GÜTER

82632 5/5 p Min. ca 3 kg 170 a 44 A □□□ Sign. 82
Each successive phase of contemporary art therefore
permeates the forms of things in everyday use, irrespec-
tive of whether they are hand-wrought or machine-made
GENERAL CHEMICALS DEPARTMENT ROCHESTER

82633 6 p Min. ca 4 kg 190 a 50 A
Le programme du lundi de Pâques comportait deux
épreuves d'obstacles, l'une plus importante et plus
difficile que l'autre, mais présentant toutes les deux
LA FRANCE ART GRAPHIQUE ET LA PUBLICITÉ

82634 8 p Min. ca 5 kg 150 a 42 A
Für die Technik ist die Erschließung neuer
Energiequellen im Hinblick auf eine stetig
steigende Konkurrenz von besonderem Wert
BAU DES NILKRAFTWERKES ASSUAN

82635 10 p /1 Bild Min. ca 6 kg 130 a 38 A □□□ Sign. 82
Blant de mange Lofotfilmer noterer vi
Lofotliv, tatt opp etter initiativ av Norsk
VINTERSPORTSSTED ST. MORITZ

82636 10 p Min. ca 6 kg 120 a 34 A
Fremdsprachliche Lehrbücher sind
wertvolle Stützen der Fachliteratur
STADTBIBLIOTHEK HANNOVER

82643 36 p Min. ca 14 kg 24 a 8A

Synchronstudio Calais

82644 48 p Min. ca 16 kg 12 a 4A

Plastics Industry

82645 60 p Min. ca 20 kg 10 a 4A

Buenos Aires

ABCDEFGHIJKLMNOPQRSTUVWXYZ
abcdefghijklmnopqrstuvwxyzß 1234567890

82637 12 p Min. ca 6 kg 78 a 24 A

Der Stand der Fernsehtechnik
FILMBERICHTE VOM TAGE

82638 14 p Min. ca 7 kg 66 a 20 A

Fastest way to start a sale
EXPORT DEPARTMENT

82639 16 p Min. ca 8 kg 58 a 18 A

Stoffe in bester Qualität
HERREN-KLEIDUNG

82640 20 p Min. ca 10 kg 48 a 14 A

Dampfschiffahrten
OSTASIENLINIE

82641 24 p Min. ca 10 kg 38 a 10 A

Arc de Triomphe

82642 28 p Min. ca 12 kg 32 a 10 A

Radiumbäder

Aus den fruchtbarsten
Gebieten Indiens, Ceylons
und Japans kommen die
bedeutendsten Teesorten
der Welt. Der Teestrauch wird
zwischen 5 und 15 m hoch
und besitzt lange schmale
Blätter. Die gereiften Blätter
werden durch uralte Aufbe-
reitungsmethoden in die
verschiedenen hocharoma-
tischen Teesorten umge-
wandelt. Der bei uns
bekannte »schwarze Tee«
wechselt seine grüne Farbe
in ein dunkles, kupferfarbe-
nes Braun und nimmt
seinen angenehmen Duft an

82477a 5/5 p Min. ca 3 kg 130 a 42 A □□□ Sign. 63
Unter den industriellen Erzeugnissen, die von Rösch
entwickelt wurden, nahmen moderne Tapeten einen
TAPETEN FÜR DIE NEUE WOHNUNG 1234567890

82478 6 p Min. ca 4 kg 130 a 46 A
In the pig-iron branch of iron and steel trade pro-
duction has by only one meaning resumed normal
CENTRAL AMERICAN RAILROAD STATION

82479 8 p Min. ca 5 kg 130 a 38 A
Die Zusammenarbeit mit der Industrie
POLYTECHNISCHE LEHRANSTALT

82481 10 p /1 Bild Min. ca 6 kg 112 a 32 A □□□ Sign. 62
Fantasiske kaktuspark i Monaco
REJSEBOG TIL SYDFRANKRIG

82482 10 p Min. ca 6 kg 106 a 30 A
Musée d'Extrème-Orient à Paris
ÉTUDE DE LA CIVILISATION

82483 12 p Min. ca 6 kg 72 a 22 A
Kraftfahrzeug-Reparaturen
AUTOMOBIL-EXPORTE

82484 14 p Min. ca 7 kg 58 a 18 A
La chronique des lettres
AGENCE DE VOYAGE

82485 16 p Min. ca 8 kg 54 a 18 A
Profileisen-Walzwerk
STAB 1234567890

82486 20 p Min. ca 13 kg 46 a 14 A

Antenna systems
RADIOSTUDIO

82487 24 p Min. ca 10 kg 34 a 10 A

Transportkran
WERKSTOFF

82488 28 p Min. ca 12 kg 30 a 8 A

Atomantrieb
ZENTRALE

82489 36 p Min. ca 14 kg 22 a 6 A

Biblioteca
PINTURA

82490 48 p Min. ca 16 kg 10 a 4 A

Scripts

82491 60 p Min. ca 20 kg 8 a 4 A

MAIN

82492 72 p Min. ca 24 kg 8 a 4 A

Buch

Größere Grade als Plakatschrift in »Paladar«

Die Akzidenz-Grotesk-Serie

Die Rückbesinnung auf hervorragende ältere
Schriftschnitte hat auch die schöne Akzidenz-
Grotesk-Serie wieder in den blickpunkt typo-
graphischer Gestaltung gestellt. Bedeutende
Industrieunternehmungen im In- und Ausland
geben diesen kleinen Schriftfamilien den Vorzug

wirtschaftlich   unentbehrlich
zeitgerecht

PRINTING PAPERS

FOR LETTERPRESS PRINTING

LITHOGRAPHY

BOOK PUBLISHING

Richmondson Ltd.

82705 5/5 p Min. ca 3 kg 264 a 66 A □□□ Sign. 84
Die Welt der Zukunft, ihre technischen Anlage, ihre Siedlungen und ihre Schönheit, sind in ihren
deutlichen Umriss in unserer Konstogkeit gepägt. So ist unser der verkehrene Röhr
EINE RELLUNGSSCHWEIGERE SOLANG VOR PROFESSOR HENRY HARTTON, WIEN

82706 6 p Min. ca 4 kg 208 a 72 A □□□ Sign. 83
Instruction and research. Industrial experiments and teamwork, will be made com-
plementary to one another; the maintenance of it just between Genotoin Interests
SAMPLE FROM A SERIE OF MAGAZINE ADVERTISEMENT IN COLOUR

82708 8 p Min. ca 5 kg 264 a 66 A
La procédé à la trame de soie est un procédé, ennuyer dans son applica-
tion, qui a prix, ven derniers années, un développement extrêmement ac-
LA TRAME DE SOIE PAR LES JAPONAIS DE L'ANTIQUITÉ 47890

82709 9/10 p Min. ca 5 kg 180 a 46 A □□□ Sign. 62
Al realizar los petróleos mexicanos el esfuerzo para concluir estas
magnas obras dentro del plazo programado, tuvo muy presente la
EL PRIMERO INSTITUTO TECNOLÓGICO DE BARCELONA

82710 10 p Min. ca 5 kg 190 a 50 A
Nach eigenen neuen Entwürfen stellen unsere Werkstätten
Stahlmöbel in den modernsten und besten Ausführungen her
DIE STEIGENDE PRODUKTION VON STAHLMÖBELN

82712 12 p Min. ca 5 kg 150 a 36 A
Dansk Boghaandværk i København / Kalundborg
KULØRT TIDSSKRIFT FOR SALG OG REKLAME

82714 14 p Min. ca 7 kg 120 a 34 A
Internationales Tennis-Turnier WIMBLEDON

82718 16 p Min. ca 8 kg 112 a 32 A
Lista de precios en Tipos y MÁQUINAS

82720 20 p Min. ca 10 kg 80 a 26 A
A Motor Tour to CHELTENHAM

82724 24 p Min. ca 10 kg 56 a 18 A
Fortschritte der TECHNIK

Helvetica – Max Miedinger – 1957

hel
ve
tica
helvetica
tica

Faceless and timeless. Eduard Hoffmann, head of the Haas Type Foundry in Münchenstein near Basel, was planning a new Grotesque in 1949. His model was Schelter Grotesque, the official Bauhaus typeface. Swiss designers at the time had started making increasing use of Akzidenz Grotesk, which then re-entered the world as 'Swiss typography'. Hoffmann knew exactly what the new typeface should look like and entrusted the design to Max Miedinger in Zurich, who was an expert on Grotesque typefaces. His sketches were discussed, assessed and corrected with Hoffmann and then passed to the in-house punch-cutting works at Haas Type foundry for casting in lead. The name of the typeface in 1957 was Neue Haas Grotesk; in 1960, the new typeface appeared from Stempel foundry called Helvetica. When Linotype adopted the new face, first for mechanical typesetting in lead and later for photosetting, they had to rework the whole design because Helvetica was never planned as a full range of mechanical and hot-metal faces. However, after the success of Univers, the highly extended type family by Adrian Frutiger that used numbers for the different members of the family, Stempel was forced to re-design the whole range of Helvetica following the same method. Helvetica Light was designed by Erich Schultz-Anker, artistic director at Stempel, in conjunction with Arthur Ritzel. In 1982, Neue Helvetica was launched by Stempel; it was just what designers were looking for: a faceless, timeless typeface.

abcdefghijklm

nopqrstuvwxyz

1234567890

(.,-:;!?'‘*[&%§)

A B C D E F G H I

J K L M N O P Q R

S T U V W X Y Z

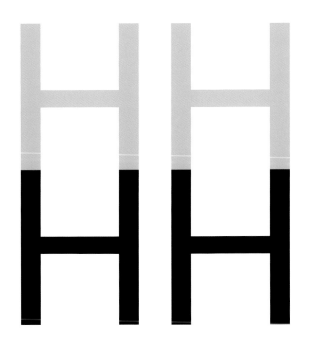

Helvetica 55 Roman

Helvetica 25 UltraLight *H*

Helvetica 35 Thin *Helvet*

45 Light *Helvetica 46*

Roman *Helvetica 56 Ita*

Helvetica 66 MediumI

Helvetica 76 BoldItali

Helvetica 86 Heavy

Black ***Helvetica***

elvetica 26 UltraLightItalic

ca 36 ThinItalic Helvetica

ightItalic Helvetica 55

c Helvetica 65 Medium

alic Helvetica 75 Bold

Helvetica 85 Heavy

Italic Helvetica 95

96 BlackItalic

FÜR DIE
ELEMENTARE
TYPO-
GRAPHIE

ist nach Aussagen ihrer
vielen Anhänger unsere
VENUS
die geeignetste Schrift

Der bekannte und be-
rühmte Bauhausmeister
L.MOHOLY-NAGY
urteilt in „Offset-, Buch-
und Werbekunst" Nr. 7:
Als Auszeichnungs-
und Titelschrift besitzen
wir dagegen annähernd
brauchbare, gute Schrif-
ten, deren geometrische
und fonetische Urform,
wie Quadrat oder Kreis,
ohne Verzerrungen zur
Geltung kommt. Das ist
die Venus-Grotesk

BAUERSCHE GIESSEREI
FRANKFURT A. MAIN W 13

FUTURA

SCHMUCK

LEIPZIG BERLIN BARCELONA MADRID BILBAO SEVILLA

BAUERSCHE
GIESSEREI
FRANKFURT-M

Futura is a timeless, elementary typeface. In 1925, Jan Tschichold published a special edition of <u>Typographische Mitteilungen</u> entitled 'Elementary Typography', in which he first formulated his efforts to create a new typography: 'Of the typefaces available, Grotesque or Black face are the nearest to what the New Typography needs, because they are simple in design and easy to read. But there is no reason why other easy-to-read typefaces should not be used. The right typeface does not yet exist.' Bauhaus leader László Moholy-Nagy published in the magazine <u>Bauhausheft 7</u> in 1926, 'Since all existing Grotesque book styles lack basic style, Grotesque still has to be created'. In the same volume Herbert Bayer's 'Attempt at a New Typeface' and Josef Albers's 'Stencil Type as Hoarding Type' also featured.

At the same time, Paul Renner was developing a new Grotesque style based on constructivist principles and on such simple basic forms as the circle, triangle and square. The first samples of the new style made their appearance in 1925. Willy Haas explained, 'With the new Futura, Paul Renner shows a non-historical, constructive solution, which looks uncommonly noble and pure, is equally at home in classical and modern uses, and despite its strict design, does not bombard us with doctrine but falls easily on the eye… So much personal style with so much abstract strength of form, such fine, human, noble mixture is not something we are used to seeing very often.'

In 1933, after the National Socialist Party seized power in Germany, Renner resigned from the Munich School for Master Book Printers and retired to Lake Geneva. In 1947, he published his book <u>Order and Harmony in Colour</u>, at the same time as his earlier book, <u>The Art of Typography</u>, was reprinted.

Futura: the typeface of its time, the typeface of our time.

Futura Schmuck, constructive and classical, 1927.

abcdefghijklm

nopqrstuvwxyz

1234567890

(. , - : ; ! ? ' ' ' * [& % §)

A B C D E F G H I

J K L M N O P Q R

S T U V W X Y Z

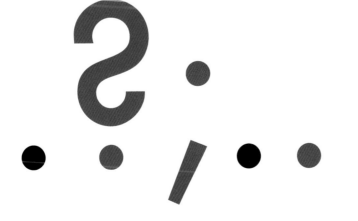

Futura

SOMMER
DER MUSIK

FRANKFURT AM MAIN
11. JUNI BIS 28. AUGUST 1927

6. WOCHE

IM BACHSAAL
TÄGLICH 16 UHR
ORGELKONZERTE

Sonntag 17. Juli	Morgenfeier des Hessischen Sängerbundes Teatro dei Piccoli, Marionettenspiele Gamelan-Orchester und Javanische Tänze Tanz- und Gesangsgruppen aus Rußland	Bachsaal 9 Uhr Bachsaal 20 U. Saxophon 17 U. Opernh. 20 Uhr
Montag 18. Juli	Tanzabend »La Argentina«, Span. Tänze Quartett »Pro Arte«, Belg. Kammermusik Teatro dei Piccoli, Marionettenspiele Gamelan-Orchester und Javanische Tänze	Opernh. 20 Uhr Beethovensaal Bachsaal 20 U. Saxophon 17 U.
Dienstag 19. Juli	Tanzabend »La Argentina«, Span. Tänze Quartett »Pro Arte«, Belg. Kammermusik Teatro dei Piccoli, Marionettenspiele Gamelan-Orchester und Javanische Tänze	Opernh. 20 Uhr Beethovensaal Bachsaal 20 U. Saxophon 17 U.
Mittwoch 20. Juli	Tanz- und Gesangsgruppen aus Rußland Teatro dei Piccoli, Marionettenspiele Gamelan-Orchester und Javanische Tänze Hausfrauen-Nachmittag mit »Küchenmusik«	Opernh. 20 Uhr Bachsaal 20 U. Saxophon 17 U. Unterhalt.-Park
Donnerstag 21. Juli	Tage für mechan. Musik, Leitg. P. Hindemith Teatro dei Piccoli, Marionettenspiele Gamelan-Orchester und Javanische Tänze Streichorchester-Konzert, Leitg. Joh. Strauß	Beethovensaal Bachsaal 20 U. Saxophon 17 U. Unterhalt.-Park
Freitag 22. Juli	Tanz- und Gesangsgruppen aus Rußland Tage für mechan. Musik, Leitg. P. Hindemith Teatro dei Piccoli, Marionettenspiele Gamelan-Orchester und Javanische Tänze	Opernh. 20 Uhr Beethovensaal Bachsaal 20 U. Saxophon 17 U.
Samstag 23. Juli	Tanz- und Gesangsgruppen aus Rußland Teatro dei Piccoli, Marionettenspiele Tage für mechan. Musik, Leitg. P. Hindemith Streichorchester-Konzert, Leitg. Joh. Strauß	Opernh. 20 Uhr Bachsaal 20 U. Beethovensaal Unterhalt.-Park

IM
UNTERHALTUNGS
PARK: JEDEN TAG
KONZERT U. TANZ

TYP: LEISTIKOW

MUSIK IM LEBEN
DER VÖLKER
INTERNAT. AUSSTELLUNG

The advertisement, 'Sommer der Musik'
('Summer of Music'), uses Futura, 1927.

Futura and Futura Schmuck, Bauersche
Giesserei Frankfurt-am-main, 1927.

'Wir geben Rabatt' ('We Give a Discount'),
1927.

WAS
BIETET
IHNEN
UNSER
FUTURA
SCHMUCK

DAS
GROSSE
RENNEN

1.-4.
AUGUST
1927

WIEN
BERLIN
PARIS

SCHRIFTLICHE ANMELDUNGEN BIS SPÄTESTENS 3. JULI FERNLEITUNG BERLIN SW 8

WIR
GEBEN
RABATT

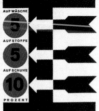

AUF WÄSCHE
5
AUF STOFFE
5
AUF SCHUHE
10
PROZENT

KAUFHAUS MERKUR

Gill Sans first appeared at the annual
congress of the British Printing
Federation in May 1928. Eric Gill was
the *enfant terrible* of typography.

FROM SCULPTOR TO TYPOGRAPHER, Arthur Eric Rowton Gill (1882–1940) trained as an architect in 1900. After he married, he joined an Arts and Crafts group in Ditchling, Sussex, where he worked as a graphic designer and illustrator and his first typeface design – Perpetua – was published in 1925. In 1928, he worked in High Wycombe as a sculptor and mason. During the same period, he and his son-in-law René Hague also ran their own hand press, publishing a number of books on industrial design and crafts. Gill's most important face is GillSans, pure and simple. Perpetua and Joanna, named after Gill's daughter and initially cast solely in 12 point specifically for his publication *Essay on Typography* (1931), were Gill's only other type designs to become established. In 1916, he was working on sculptures at Westminster Station and was asked to design a simple, geometric typeface to be used for all signage and directions on the London Underground. In the design, he retained classical proportions in such letters as the 'g', but for the 'R' he used his preferred character with its elegant down-sweeping tail. In October 1926, a Bristol book dealer, Douglas Cleverdon, asked Gill to paint a sign in the style of sans-serif lettering, and a few weeks later, Stanley Morison, artistic adviser to the Monotype Corporation, visited Cleverdon and noticed the sign. He was convinced that Gill could design a similar a sans-serif face for Monotype. Up until that point, Gill had only used capitals, so it was no surprise that the first drawings of the lowercase letters were quite different from the face that was finally cast. Monotype helped with many of the improvements and, in 1928, Gill became an adviser to Monotype. When GillSans first appeared at the end of the 1920s, it was not what the British print establishment had been looking for. Its reception was similar to that of Futura in Germany, where comments on Paul Renner's design had referred to it as a fashion that would soon be forgotten. The first version of GillSans was finished for the annual congress of the British Printing Federation in May 1928, where Stanley Morison gave an address and the invitations were set in the new face. FROM THEN ON, GILLSANS WAS A WINNER.

abcdefghijklm

nopqrstuvwxyz

1234567890

(.,-:;!?'' '*[&%§)

A B C D E F G H I

J K L M N O P Q R

S T U V W X Y Z

GillSans

Letterproof set in Gill medium by
Johan Enschede & Zonen, 1968.

GILL NORMAAL

ABCDEFG
HIJKLMN
OPQRST
UVWXYZ
1234567
890
&

GILL NORMAAL

abcdefghij
klmnopq
rstuvw
xyzij
.,:;!?''-(*—

Top spread

Similarly, the modern printer never grieves over sending to the bin a fount of very durable (and hence expensive) type that shows no signs of wear. He asks "does it show any sign of being any use to us?" Often he gets the ridiculous answer: "No, but it's perfectly good type." It may be *perfect* as type, but customers have called it *no good*.

Thus balancing the true elements of the problem, the modern printer calculates *how soon* he can hurry a display fount back to its most potential state: liquidity. He hopes it will be very soon, for that will show that the fount has been at work. He knows he has waited too long if he has paid a penny more on make-ready than he would have paid to re-cast it. It is actually more expensive, in many cases, to make-ready than to *have-ready*.

Skilled labour costs the modern printer more than it cost his father, metal costs him less, and father's best display faces are serious museum pieces in his type book. Above all, his father's mental image of a type *buyer*. He, the son, is a type *maker*, so he knows better. He makes movable type, partly because he *can* do it, but chiefly for other and stronger reasons. He has display cases, but not necessarily as the place to which used type is to be returned.

It is interesting to see a modern printer distinguished (mentally) from his father by his greater interest in what type-metal *becomes* than in what frozen types *are*. It is even more interesting to see how the word "face" has ceased to refer to the visible face of a given type, and has come to mean "principle of design governing the whole fount"—*any* fount that is an example of that face. Still more significant, still more "modern", is the idea of the "live" Type Repertory, of which any given face is only one example. The old-fashioned Type Book was a jumble, the repository of anything the printer had happened to acquire. The modern one is a balanced, planned repertory, subject to frequent changes until it is flexible enough to fill all reasonable requirements. In display, where the great effort is to be "different" from the rival display, one cannot even *take a stand* (again that metaphor!) as to the adequacy of any given range: hence the really modern idea of hiring display matrices in order to *keep pace* with changes of style without *tying up* too much capital in matrices of an ephemeral design.

Again and again these instances have shown one other characteristic of our age: the tendency to "plan" rather than to "let things happen". But that is only another way

6

of saying that the interest is shifting from what a thing happens to be at a given moment, to what is going to become of it, in time, and under the control of that all-important "invisible force", human reason and will power.

Thus the essentially "modern" composing room is one in which the philosopher Heraclitus would find a dozen illustrations of his principle that "everything flows"—that the eye perceives solid objects at any given moment, but that the mind perceives the "fluid" principle of change, growth or decay, behind them. Metal in flux; flexibility in the type repertory (and in corrections as well); a "plan" by which the *flow* of work is regulated to keep slack time productive and rush time free from stoppages, and a general willingness to "move with the times", even if it means going out of one's way to find new markets and understand the new needs of "planned marketing"—and if it means sparing the apprentices so that they can be trained for the new age—all these are fairly new tendencies, and all depend far more upon *intellectual insight*, far less upon mere observation, than the older ways.

A TRULY MODERN TYPE FACE

The column below is set in 10 pt. "Monotype" Times New Roman 327, showing the original short descenders. The column on the left is set in 12 pt. of the same series, cast on 14 pt., with special long-descender characters g j p q y f ʃ j p q y substituted. The marginal notes are in 8 pt. on 9 pt. with the special long descenders. Note the remarkable ease with which this "news face" can thus be transformed into a classic "book face" when economy of space is less imperative. *This is the 11 pt. with long descenders, on 12 pt.*

MONOTYPE GILL SANS

CONSPECTUS

353

Bottom spread

Display mustPAY the MODERN Way

No chance for Costly founts To-day

All English display sizes to 72. Also Composition 8, 10 & 12 & Didot 72

EXTRA BOLD SERIES NUMBER 321

1234567890 £&?!-;:,.

262. 72

'Beauty looks

CONTINUING THE STORY OF "MONOTYPE" GILL SANS

A series of L.N.E.R. advertisements, 11-inch doubles in The Times, was a prelude to the second phase in the history of Gill Sans. Here the titling letter was used in conjunction with a deliberately-contrasted lower-case, large Blado italic.

Meanwhile a lower-case Gill was being cut; and from the very first there was present in the minds of the cutters a potential purpose which goes far to explain the extraordinary usefulness of the face.

The lower-case was disciplined from its very cradle by severe casts. Any element of design such as prettiness or originality, which would count for much in marketing a display face, had to pass the sterner tests that are given to a face before it is chosen

9 pt.

for standardizing texts and display alike. Any whimsicality that would become wearisome had already been jettisoned; now the problem was to guard against anything which would interfere with quick **readability in small sizes**—however successful it might be in display sizes. The L.N.E.R. standardization to "Monotype" Gill Sans was the first of many standardizations (some on the same huge scale) to the same face. The historical importance of the first is that it was practically decided upon while the basic elements of the Gill Sans combination fount were still being cut in the smaller time-table sizes.

Several sizes were in fact cut to order, and recut if they did not fulfil the very exacting requirements of the time-table reader.

[continued overleaf]

72 & 60 point

are for Casting on A 'MONOTYPE' SUPER Caster. Sizes from 48 pt

down may be cast on any "Monotype" composition caster equipped with Display Attachment

Above: Bold Condensed. This line, Heavy 275.

.,:;-!?&£ 1234567890

GILL SANS

231 TITLING BOLD

ABCDEFGHIJKLMN
OPQRSTUVWXYZ

The quickest face for glance reading; Stripped for ACTion

These are some display sizes of 'MONOTYPE' GILL SANS 362: LIGHT

after herself'

THE WORD MONOTYPE is the Registered Trade Mark of The Monotype Corporation Limited

"Monotype" Gill Outline, Series No. 290

'MONOTYPE'
DISPLAY MATRICES (14 PT. UP) MAY BE HIRED BY THE DAY

Above: Outline Titling, Series No. 304, 36 pt.

"DISPLAY"

GILL CAMEO RULED

VARIANTS

TimesNewRoman – Stanley Morison – 1932

'If I can', said William Morris,
and Utopia became a reality.

SEARCHING FOR THE BEST POSSIBLE TYPEFACE FOR A NEWSPAPER.

Stanley Ignatius Arthur Morison (1889–1967) became typographic advisor to Monotype in 1923, where he was in charge of designing typeface families based on historical models. The manager of *The Times*, William Lints-Smith, had heard that Morison had been very scathing about the out-dated typography of the newspaper. They met and after a long discussion Morison advised Lints-Smith to re-design *The Times* from scratch. Morison became typographical adviser for the newspaper and produced several test pages in different type-faces, including Baskerville, Plantin, Imprint, Ionic and a version of Perpetua. At that time, Linotype in the USA was producing a series of typefaces, such as Ionic, for setting long texts. Excelsior followed in 1931 and is still one of the most popular newspaper typefaces. After several presentations, Morison decided that a completely new typeface was needed, and, in 1931, he presented two designs: an overhauled Perpetua and a modernized Plantin. The committee of *The Times* decided on the second option and Times New Roman was born, making its first appearance on 3 October 1932. It remains today a much-used typeface and, thanks to its wide-reaching distribution and marketing, it is set to survive.

a b c d e f g h i j k l m

n o p q r s t u v w x y z

1 2 3 4 5 6 7 8 9 0

(. , - : ; ! ? ' ' * [& % §)

A B C D E F G H I

J K L M N O P Q R

S T U V W X Y Z

TNR

TimesNewRomanPS

SPECIMENS OF 'MONOTYPE'

Times New Roman

AND ITS RELATED SERIES

designed, tested and commissioned by

THE ❧ TIMES

OF LONDON

The Monotype Corporation Limited

was entrusted by *The Times* with the task of cutting the thousands of patterns and steel punches required for the experimental and final versions of this renowned face. *The Times* New Roman Series 327, with its related bolds, italics, etc., and no fewer than five series of related titlings, was approved and adopted by *The Times* in 1931. One year later, The Monotype Corporation Ltd. was permitted to place on the market the entire family (of 12 series, totalling almost 70 different founts) of this face which has been called "THE MOST IMPORTANT NEW TYPE DESIGN OF THE TWENTIETH CENTURY".

Specimens of Monotype's Times New Roman, the most important type design of the twentieth century. The new front page of *The Times*, 1932.

THE  TIMES

Nº 45,977   **LATE LONDON EDITION**   LONDON, MONDAY, OCTOBER 3, 1932   **PRICE 2d**

BIRTHS

MARRIAGES

DEATHS

IN MEMORIAM
ON ACTIVE SERVICE

MOTOR-CAR HIRE SERVICE

ROAD TRANSPORT

RIDING AND SHOOTING

SPORT AND GARDEN

HOSPITAL NURSES

PERSONAL

PERSONAL (continued)

CLOTHES VALETING

AGENCIES

BUSINESS OFFERS

DIRECTORS AND PARTNERS

INVESTMENTS AND LOANS

KENNEL, FARM, AND AVIARY

DOGS

WANTED

FARM

EDUCATIONAL

A SOUND BUSINESS EDUCATION

THE GREGG SCHOOLS

GABBITAS, THRING & CO.

SECRETARIAL COLLEGE

TRUMAN & KNIGHTLEY, LTD.

N. W. ROSS, M.A.

SCHOOLS

MISS MABEL HAWTREY

SCHOOLFINDERS, LTD.

KENSINGTON COLLEGE

ST. JAMES'S SECRETARIAL COLLEGE

MEDICAL SCHOOLS

MIDDLESEX HOSPITAL MEDICAL SCHOOL
LONDON W.

CONTINENTAL EDUCATION

INSTITUTION NOTRE-DALE

CLUB ANNOUNCEMENTS

ABBEY & NAVY CLUB

THE FISHERY CLUB

HURST PARK CLUB

BATH RACE CLUB

ASTON CLINTON PARK, BUCKS.

ASTON CLINTON GOLF CLUB

DANCE AND THEATRE CLUBS

AMATEUR DANCERS' CLUB

DANCING

YOUR REQUIREMENTS

INDEX TO CLASSIFIED ADVERTISEMENTS INCLUDING SCALE OF CHARGES

MANUALE

TIPOGRAFICO

DEL CAVALIÈRE

GIAMBATTISTA BODONI

VOLUME PRIMO.

PARMA

PRESSO LA VEDOVA

MDCCCXVIII.

PAPALE

Quousq;
tandem
abutêre,
Catilina,

SALUZZO

Bodoni by Bodoni [above].
Bodoni Linotype [below left].
Bodoni Monotype [below right].

LINOTYPE

Quosq;
tandem
abutêre,
Catilina,

BODONI

MONOTYPE

Quosq;
tandem
abutêre,
Catilina,

BODONI

GIAMBATTISTA BODONI ADVISED THAT TO BE SURE

of a product fit for a king, there must be lots of white space and generous line spacing and the type size should not be too miserly. Bodoni has been called the king of printers and the printer of kings, and this reputation is the result of the *Manuale Typografico*, a compilation of his life's work, which was published after his death in 1818 in Parma by his widow Margherita Bodoni. The first copy was dedicated to Her Royal Highness Marie-Louise, Princess of Parma. This handbook on the art of book printing consisted of 546 pages showing a total of 665 different alphabets, including 100 exotic typefaces, 1,300 vignettes and 170 Latin scripts, some of which used up to 380 matrices. The edition had a very small print run, some sources say as few as 150 copies, while others state 290. According to his widow, Bodoni made, corrected and cast over 55,000 matrices in 50 years. Bodoni was particularly interested in design and page harmony in terms of the choice and size of the typeface, the leading and the interplay of line length, spacing and column width. The relationship between black and white and the generous use of space also played major roles. The typeface Bodoni has a long history: there is a Bodoni by Morris Fuller Benton for ATF (1907), then followed a version by Monotype and then one by Haas Type Foundry in Switzerland (1924). Haas Bodoni was copied by the Amsterdam type foundry Berthold, Stempel, Linotype and Ludlow, while Johannes Wagner introduced a new Bodoni in 1961. There are more than 500 Bodonis in the world. In this book, there are two beautiful examples: Filosofia by Zuzana Licko (1996, see p. 222) and Gianotten by Antonio Pace (1999, see p. 166).

a b c d e f g h i j k l m

n o p q r s t u v w x y z

1 2 3 4 5 6 7 8 9 0

(. , - : ; ! ? ' ' * [& % §)

A B C D E F G H I

J K L M N O P Q R

S T U V W X Y Z

chic
ago

Bodoni

Anker-Teppiche

errangen ihren Weltruf ohne Reklame, nur allein durch ihre große Haltbarkeit, Farbenechtheit, Musterschönheit wie auch Preiswürdigkeit. Deshalb empfehlen wir die Anker-Teppiche

ANKER-TEPPICHE HALTEN – WAS DER ANKER VERSPRICHT

Two pages from *Bodonischriften*,
D. Stempel AG, c. 1932.

Où passer la soirée?

Suivez le conseil de....

H. André-Legrand (Comoedia)

«Nous irons aux 'Miracles' voir ce film superficiel et ravissant qui ressemble à des vacances.»

Jean Chataignier (Le Journal)

«Votre soirée ne sera pas perdue si vous décidez d'aller vous amuser au Congrès, aussi bien et aussi follement que le congrès s'amuse.»

Michel Ferry (Le Micro)

«Un rêve exquis. Laissez-vous tenter par son charme.»

R. de Lafforest (L'Ami du Peuple)

«Quand un tel film est projeté sur un écran parisien, on n'a plus le droit de dire que l'on ne sait que faire de sa soirée.»

Jean Fayard (Candide)

«Je suis certain que vous prendrez un très vif plaisir à ce spectacle.»

Paul Reboux (Paris-Midi)

«Je ne crois pas abuser de votre confiance en vous engageant à aller voir 'Le Congrès s'amuse'.»

....et allez voir

Le Congrès s'amuse

Edité par l'Alliance Cinématographique Européenne (Production U.F.A.)

aux Miracles!

Logotype for Le Musée d'Orsay, Paris, by
Bruno Monguzzi and Jean Widmer, 1990.

Poster by Philippe Apeloig for the
exhibition 'Chicago, images d'une
métropole 1872–1922', Le Musée
d'Orsay, Paris, 1987.

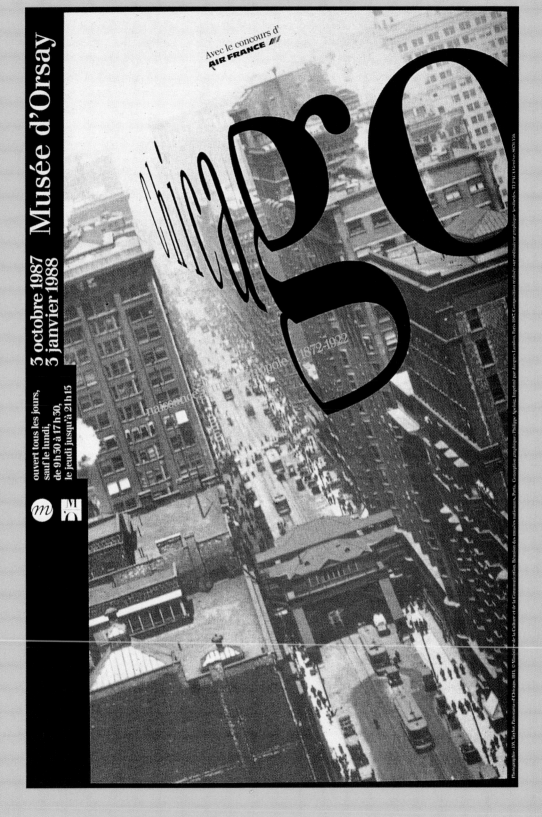

Musée d'Orsay

3 octobre 1987
3 janvier 1988

ouvert tous les jours,
sauf le lundi,
de 9 h 30 à 17 h 30,
le jeudi jusqu'à 21 h 15

Avec le concours d'
AIR FRANCE

Chicago

1872-1922

JOHN BASKERVILLE
From the portrait after Miller in the National Portrait Gallery, London
Photograph by Messrs. Emery Walker, Ltd.

THE
BASKERVILLE TYPES
A CRITIQUE

I

There are three kinds of roman type which the book printer can use in England: Old Face, Modern—and Baskerville. And recently there has been a tendency to hold that the greatest of these is Baskerville. It is not a compromise between the Old Face and modern designs, any more than to be twenty-five is a compromise between being twenty and being thirty. Baskerville is something in itself, something remarkably engaging, finished and equal to the occasion. In these pages an effort will be made to find the reasons, æsthetic and structural, for the unique charm of the Baskerville letter; to indicate what its appeal was to the eighteenth century, and what it will most probably be to the present time. For intelligent as became the appreciation of Baskerville's design soon after his time, it is not impossible, indeed there is every indication, that its permanent adoption as a standard face (and perhaps *the* standard face) will date from our own day.

A "transitional" style in any art is by its very definition, one which is superseded by something that carries its beauties a step further. But the fact remains that beauty is not always the better for being worked out to the last thread of obvious consistency, for being as it were segregated under glass; and

3

A QUEST FOR THE BEST RESULT
John Baskerville (1706–75)

John Baskerville began cutting and casting his own typefaces in 1754 and was influenced by the lettering of stonemasons, as were other English type designers who later went on to produce the typefaces we regard as typically English today: the Clarendons, Grotesques and Egyptians. Baskerville sought to improve the quality of English printing and typography and paid great attention to every element of the printing process from papers to inks and from typefaces to printing machines.

In 1750, Baskerville established a paper mill, type foundry and printing business, producing his first book in 1757. He also printed many of John Milton's works, but his most famous publication is *Juvenalis* in 1761. Baskerville invented coated paper when he was working as a printer for the University of Cambridge. Such elements as Baskerville's use of an open way of typesetting to increase the spacing between words and lines and the width on the page, his use of coated paper and his very black ink made him famous throughout Europe. After Baskerville's death, a large part of his materials, his secret ink formula and his method of producing coated paper were sold to the Frenchman Caron de Beaumarchais, who printed, with the Baskerville letters, a publication consisting of 70 volumes of Voltaire (1785–89). Baskerville would have been proud of the results.

a b c d e f g h i j k l m

n o p q r s t u v w x y z

1 2 3 4 5 6 7 8 9 0

(. , - : ; ! ? ' ' * [& % §)

ABCDEFGHI

JKLMNOPQR

STUVWXYZ

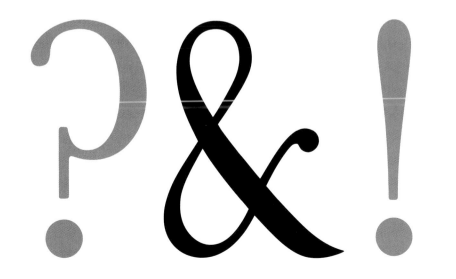

?&!

Baskerville Book

Title page and page from *A Specimen of Printing Letters Designed by John Baskerville*, Monotype, 1926.

SPECIMEN

By *JOHN BASKERVILLE* of BIRMINGHAM,

In the County of Warwick, *Letter-Founder and Printer.*

To CNEIUS PLANCIUS.

I Am indebted to you for two letters, dated from Corcyra. You congratulate me in one of them on the account you have received, that I ftill preferve my former authority in the commonwealth: and wifh me joy in the other of my late marriage. With refpect to the firft, if to mean well to the intereft of my country and to approve that meaning to eve-ry friend of its liberties, may be confidered as maintaining my authority; the account you have heard is certainly true. But if it confifts in rendering thofe fentiments effectual to the public welfare, or at leaft in daring freely to fupport

To *CAIUS CASSIUS*, proquæftor.

MY own inclinations have anticipated your recommendation: and I have long fince received Marcus Fabius into the number of my friends. He has extremely endeared himfelf to me indeed, by his great politenefs and elegance of manners: but particularly by the fingu-lar affection I have obferved he bears towards you. Accordingly, tho' your letter in his behalf was not without effect, yet my own knowledge of the regard he entertains for you had fomewhat more: you may be affured therefore I fhall very faithfully confer upon him the good offi-ces you requeft.

TO THE PUBLIC.

JOHN BASKERVILLE propofes, by the advice and affiftance of feveral learned men, to print, from the Cambridge edition corrected with all poffible care, an elegant edition of Virgil. The work will be printed in quarto, on a very fine writing royal paper, and with the above letter. The price of the Volume in fheets will be one guinea, no part of which will be required till the book is de-livered. It will be put to prefs as foon as the number of Subfcribers fhall amount to five hundred, whofe names will be prefixt to the work. All perfons who are inclined to encourage the undertaking, are defired to fend their names to JOHN BASKERVILLE in Birmingham; who will give fpecimens of the work to all who are defirous of feeing them.

Subfcriptions are alfo taken in, and fpecimens delivered by Meffieurs R. and J. DODSLEY, Bookfellers in Pall Mall, London. MDCCLIV.

THIRTY-SIX POINT

BASKERVILLE
ABCDEFGHIJKLMNOPQRS
TUVWXYZ

ABCDEFGHIJKLMNOPQRST

abcdefghijklmnopqrstuvwxyz

1234567890

abcdefghijklmnopqrstuvwxyz

1234567890

THIRTY POINT

Of all the occupations
  A beggar's is the best
For whenever he's a-weary
  He can lay him down to rest
So a-begging we will go

29

Caslon – William Caslon – 1725

CASLON, A MAN WITH A VERSATILE MIND.

William Caslon was born in Cradley, Worcestershire in 1692. At 13, he was apprenticed to an engraver in London and, in 1717, he became a citizen of London. In 1718, he set up independently as an engraver and two years later opened his own type foundry. The bookbinder John Watts employed Caslon to design and cast typefaces for his book covers, one of which caught the eye of William Bowyen, a well-known London printer. Bowyen and Caslon became friends and Bowyen introduced Caslon to other London printers; this was the start of one of the most successful type foundries in England. Initially, Caslon was supported financially by Watts, Bowyen and his son-in-law James Bettenham, also a printer. In his first year of business in the type foundry, Caslon produced a new typeface for printing a bible in Arabic for the Society for the Propagation of Christian Knowledge. On completion of the job, he printed a sample page of the Arabic script to sell the typeface to other printers. The sheet bore his name in roman letters designed specifically for the advertisement. This was the beginning of the popular typeface we now know as Caslon Old Face. Caslon went on to cut a number of non-roman and exotic typefaces, such as Coptic, Armenian, Etruscan, Hebrew and Caslon Gothic, his version of Black Letter. All these typefaces appeared before he published his first and extensive catalogue for his type foundry in 1734, which featured a total of 38 typefaces. Caslon's type foundry eventually moved to the famous Chriswell Street Foundry, where Caslon's son and several generations of the family ran the business for more than 120 years. In 1749, King George II made him a Justice of the Peace for the County of Middlesex. He retired and died at his country house in Bethnal Green in 1766, aged 74. A success story of an extraordinary engraver.

a b c d e f g h i j k l m

n o p q r s t u v w x y z

1 2 3 4 5 6 7 8 9 0

(. , - : ; ! ? ' ' * [& % §)

ABCDEFGHI

JKLMNOPQR

STUVWXYZ

f g j

Caslon Regular

Caslon series 60 is displayed here with a two-colour initial, Joh. Enschede & Zonen (1910).

'Caslon versus Baskerville', a Linotype Caslon advertisement, c. 1900.

Three advertisements for Kunstgewerbemuseum Berlin, Cinema Odeon Zurich and Perrot Duval & Cie in Geneva. The popularity of the Caslon revival is evident in the host of imitations that appeared.

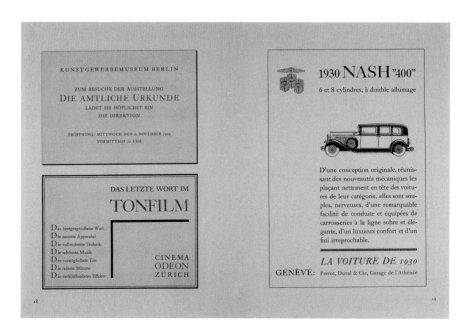

CASLON *versus* BASKERVILLE

ASLON'S only rival as a typefounder was John Baskerville, of Birmingham. Benjamin Franklin, in the following letter to Baskerville, explains in an amusing manner the difficulty even connoisseurs find in comparing the work of the two typefounders: "Let me give you a pleasing instance of the prejudice some have entertained against your work. Soon after I returned, discoursing with a gentleman concerning the artists of Birmingham, he said you would be the means of blinding all the readers of the nation, for the strokes of your letters, being too thin and narrow, hurt the eye, and he could never read a line

SPECIFICATIONS: 24 Point Caslon Old Face, 3 point leaded; Decoration, 96 Point Caslon Initial, X-1269; Second Color, X-1271. The decorative panel enclosing this page was built up with the following Linotype material: Beginning at the outside is a combination of 12 Point Border Nos. 1024, 1027 and 1028, followed by double Oxford Rule cast from 8 Point Matrix Slide No. 735. The next two units are cast from 5 Point Matrix Slide No. 406. The Oxford Rule forming the fifth and seventh units is from 6 Point Matrix Slide No. 516 with a unit composed of 18 Point Border No. 723 and Cornerpiece No. 723¼ between them. The inside unit which completes the pattern is cast from 6 Point Matrix Slide No. 1467.

L'histoire

DE THVCYDIDE ATHE.
nié, de la guerre qui fut entre les Pe.
loponesiens & Atheniés, Trãsla.
téc en lãgue Francoyse par feu
Meßire Claude de Seyßel
lors Euesque de Mar-
seille, & depuis Ar
cheuesque de
Turin.

Imprimé a Paris par Pierre Gaultier pour
Iehan Barbé & Claude Garamont.

1 5 4 5.

THE FRENCH RENAISSANCE ANTIQUA SEES THE LIGHT OF DAY.
Claude Garamond (1480–1561) was taught his craft at a young age by his
father and family members. He claimed that he could cut printed stamps
in Cicero size (12 point) at the age of fifteen. In the first quarter of the 16th
century, the counterparts of the French type cutters and printers were the
Italian creators of the Renaissance Antiqua. Aldus Manutius and
Francesco Griffo's Antiqua typefaces reached France as did the
typefaces of Pietro Bembo. Claude Garamond is one of the type cutters
and casters who created the French Renaissance Antiqua and Italica. At
that time, roman capitals and Carolingian lowercase letters were brought
together. In centralized France, conditions were more favourable for
making progress in typography and letterpress than in Italy or Germany.
Garamond's fame and position as royal type caster came after the so-called
'Grecs du Roy', which King François I, a supporter of letterpress, engaged
him to cut in 1543. The first Antiqua, which can be attributed to
Garamond, was a large typeface that appeared in EUSEBIUS and
other publications by Robert Estiennes in 1544. Title pages
after 1545 show that Garamond published either alone
or with Pierre Caultier and Jean Barbé. An
example of a modern Garamond is Jan
Tschichold's Sabon, or, even better,
the Sabon Next of Jean
François Porchez. The
circle is never
ending.

abcdefghijklm

nopqrstuvwxyz

1234567890

(.,-:;!?'`*[&%§)

ABCDEFGHI

JKLMNOPQR

STUVWXYZ

ABC

Garamond by Claude Garamond (1543) was widely seized on by typeface manufacturers as the basis for their own products.

Pages 386–87: Design attributed to Claude Garamond, 1545. Note the narrowing type and widely spaced numbers.

THIRTY-SIX POINT

I regard that man as devoid of understanding who rests capable of taunting another *with his poverty or of valuing himself on having been born in affluence.*

24

A B C D E F G
H I L M N O P
Q Qu R S T V X
X W Æ Œ abc d
e f g h i j l m n o p q
s f t u v x y z à á æ ã ct
c ĕ è ff fi fl í ò ŏ õ ô œ fi
ff ft u &

N.B.

As a contribution towards the revival of old
styles which characterizes the printing of our
day The Lanston Monotype Corporation,
Ltd., in addition to reproducing the Garamond type for the first time in Europe, has cut
a series of special italic ligatured characters,
swash letters & special "final" sorts which
will be valuable in instances where it is desired
to create a very definite antique character.
A number of these forms have for generations
been unobtainable from any source,
whether English, Continental
or American. A display
will be found on the
following
page

GARAMONT

EEN DER FRAAISTE LETTERS, DIE OOIT WERD GESNEDEN

GARAMONT

13 Corpsen

HALFVETTE GARAMONT

12 Corpsen

GARAMONT CURSIEF

10 Corpsen

LETTERGIETERIJ „AMSTERDAM"

VOORHEEN N. TETTERODE

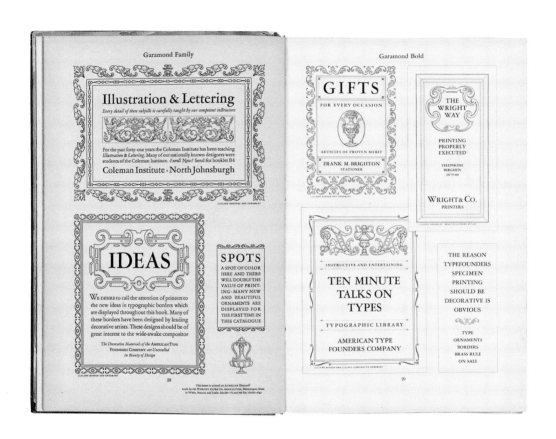

'LETTERS ARE SYMBOLS WHICH TURN MATTER INTO SPIRIT.'

Alphonse de la Martine

Typeface Index

389

Franklin, 2004
David Berlow
ITC Franklin-Black
ITC Franklin-Bold
ITC Franklin-Light
ITC Franklin-Regular
ITC FranklinComp-Black
ITC FranklinComp-Bold
ITC FranklinComp-Light
ITC FranklinComp-Regular
ITC FranklinCond-Black
ITC FranklinCond-Bold
ITC FranklinCond-Light
ITC FranklinCond-Regular
ITC FranklinNarrow-Black
ITC FranklinNarrow-Bold
ITC FranklinNarrow-Light
ITC FranklinNarrow-Regular

Demos, 2004
Gerard Unger
Demos™ Medium
Demos™ Medium SC
Demos™ Medium Italic
Demos™ Semi Bold

Praxis, 2004
Gerard Unger
Praxis™ Light
Praxis™ Light SC
Praxis™ Regular
Praxis™ Regular SC
Praxis™ Semi Bold
Praxis™ Bold
Praxis™ Heavy

Zapfino, 2003
Hermann Zapf
Zapfino™ Extra One
Zapfino™ Extra Forte One
Zapfino™ Extra Two
Zapfino™ Extra Three
Zapfino™ Extra Four
Zapfino™ Extra SmallCaps
Zapfino™ Extra Ligatures
Zapfino™ Extra Forte Alternate

Kosmik, 2002
Erik van Blokland
FF Kosmik-BoldOne
FF Kosmik-BoldThree
FF Kosmik-BoldTwo
FF Kosmik-Glyphs
FF Kosmik-PlainOne
FF Kosmik-PlainThree
FF Kosmik-PlainTwo

Beowolf, 1990
Just van Rossum,
Erik van Blokland
Beowolf Serif R21
Beowolf Serif R22
Beowolf Serif R23

Sabon Next, 2002
Jean François Porchez
Sabon™ Next Display
Sabon™ Next Display SC
Sabon™ Next Display OsF
Sabon™ Next Display Alternate
Sabon™ Next Italic Display
Sabon™ Next Italic Display SC
Sabon™ Next Italic Display OsF
Sabon™ Next Italic Display
	Alternate
Sabon™ Next Regular
Sabon™ Next Regular SC
Sabon™ Next Regular OsF
Sabon™ Next Regular Alternate
Sabon™ Next Italic
Sabon™ Next Italic SC
Sabon™ Next Italic OsF
Sabon™ Next Italic Alternate
Sabon™ Next Demi
Sabon™ Next Demi SC
Sabon™ Next Demi OsF
Sabon™ Next Demi Alternate
Sabon™ Next Demi Italic
Sabon™ Next Demi Italic SC
Sabon™ Next Demi Italic OsF
Sabon™ Next Demi Italic Alternate
Sabon™ Next Bold
Sabon™ Next Bold SC
Sabon™ Next Bold OsF
Sabon™ Next Bold Alternate
Sabon™ Next Bold Italic
Sabon™ Next Bold Italic SC
Sabon™ Next Bold Italic OsF

Sabon™ Next Bold Italic Alternate
Sabon™ Next Extra Bold
Sabon™ Next Extra Bold SC
Sabon™ Next Extra Bold OsF
Sabon™ Next Extra Bold Alternate
Sabon™ Next Extra Bold Italic
Sabon™ Next Extra Bold Italic SC
Sabon™ Next Extra Bold Italic OsF
Sabon™ Next Extra Bold Italic
	Alternate
Sabon™ Next Black
Sabon™ Next Black Alternate
Sabon™ Next Black Italic
Sabon™ Next Black Italic OsF
Sabon™ Next Black OsF
Sabon™ Next Black Italic
	Alternate

Le Monde, 1997
Jean François Porchez
Le Monde Courrier Normal
Le Monde Courrier Normal Old
	Style Figures
Le Monde Courrier Normal Small
	Caps
Le Monde Courrier Italic
Le Monde Courrier Italic Old Style
	Figures
Le Monde Courrier Italic Small
	Caps
Le Monde Courrier Demi
Le Monde Courrier Demi Old Style
	Figures
Le Monde Courrier Demi Small
	Caps
Le Monde Courrier Demi Italic
Le Monde Courrier Demi Italic Old
	Style Figures
Le Monde Courrier Demi Italic
	Small Caps
Le Monde Courrier Bold
Le Monde Courrier Bold Old Style
	Figures
Le Monde Courrier Bold Small Caps
Le Monde Courrier Bold Italic
Le Monde Courrier Bold Italic Old
	Style Figures
Le Monde Courrier Bold Italic
	Small Caps
Le Monde Livre Normal

Le Monde Livre Normal Old Style
    Figures
Le Monde Livre Normal Small Caps
Le Monde Livre Italic
Le Monde Livre Italic Old Style
    Figures
Le Monde Livre Italic Small Caps
Le Monde Livre Demi
Le Monde Livre Demi Old Style
    Figures
Le Monde Livre Demi Small Caps
Le Monde Livre Demi Italic
Le Monde Livre Demi Italic Old
    Style Figures
Le Monde Livre Demi Italic Small
    Caps
Le Monde Livre Bold
Le Monde Livre Bold Old Style
    Figures
Le Monde Livre Bold Small Caps
Le Monde Livre Bold Italic
Le Monde Livre Bold Italic Old
    Style Figures
Le Monde Livre Bold Italic Small
    Caps
Le Monde Livre Classic Regular
Le Monde Livre Classic Small Caps
Le Monde Livre Classic Alternates
Le Monde Livre Classic Italic
Le Monde Livre Classic Swashes
Le Monde Livre Classic Italic
    Alternates
Le Monde Livre Classic Bold
Le Monde Livre Classic Bold
    Alternates
Le Monde Livre Classic Vignettes
Le Monde Journal Normal
Le Monde Journal Normal Old Style
    Figures
Le Monde Journal Normal Small
    Caps
Le Monde Journal Italic
Le Monde Journal Italic Old Style
    Figures
Le Monde Journal Italic Small Caps
Le Monde Journal Demi
Le Monde Journal Demi Old Style
    Figures
Le Monde Journal Demi Small Caps
Le Monde Journal Demi Italic

Le Monde Journal Demi Italic Old
    Style Figures
Le Monde Journal Demi Italic
    Small Caps
Le Monde Journal Bold
Le Monde Journal Bold Old Style
    Figures
Le Monde Journal Bold Small Caps
Le Monde Journal Bold Italic
Le Monde Journal Bold Italic Old
    Style Figures
Le Monde Journal Bold Italic Small
    Caps
Le Monde Journal Ipa Normal
Le Monde Journal Ipa Alternates
Le Monde Journal Normal
Le Monde Journal Normal Small
    Caps
Le Monde Journal Normal Old Style
    Figures
Le Monde Sans Extra Light
Le Monde Sans Extra Light Old
    Style Figures
Le Monde Sans Extra Light Italic
Le Monde Sans Extra Light Italic
    Old Style Figures
Le Monde Sans Light
Le Monde Sans Light Old Style
    Figures
Le Monde Sans Light Italic
Le Monde Sans Light Italic Old
    Style Figures
Le Monde Sans Normal
Le Monde Sans Normal Old Style
    Figures
Le Monde Sans Normal Small Caps
Le Monde Sans Italic
Le Monde Sans Italic Old Style
    Figures
Le Monde Sans Italic Small Caps
Le Monde Sans Demi
Le Monde Sans Demi Old Style
    Figures
Le Monde Sans Demi Small Caps
Le Monde Sans Demi Italic
Le Monde Sans Demi Italic Old
    Style Figures
Le Monde Sans Demi Italic Small
    Caps
Le Monde Sans Bold

Le Monde Sans Bold Old Style
    Figures
Le Monde Sans Bold Small Caps
Le Monde Sans Bold Italic
Le Monde Sans Bold Italic Old
    Style Figures
Le Monde Sans Bold Italic Small
    Caps
Le Monde Sans Extra Bold
Le Monde Sans Extra Bold Old
    Style Figures
Le Monde Sans Extra Bold Italic
Le Monde Sans Extra Bold Italic
    Old Style Figures
Le Monde Sans Black
Le Monde Sans Black Old Style
    Figures
Le Monde Sans Black Italic
Le Monde Sans Black Italic Old
    Style Figures

Syntax, 2000
Hans Eduard Meier
Linotype Syntax™ Light
Linotype Syntax™ Light SC
Linotype Syntax™ Light OsF
Linotype Syntax™ Light Italic
Linotype Syntax™ Light Italic SC
Linotype Syntax™ Light Italic OsF
Linotype Syntax™ Regular
Linotype Syntax™ Regular SC
Linotype Syntax™ Regular OsF
Linotype Syntax™ Regular Italic
Linotype Syntax™ Italic SC
Linotype Syntax™ Regular Italic
    OsF
Linotype Syntax™ Medium
Linotype Syntax™ Medium SC
Linotype Syntax™ Medium OsF
Linotype Syntax™ Medium Italic
Linotype Syntax™ Medium Italic
    SC
Linotype Syntax™ Medium Italic
    OsF
Linotype Syntax™ Bold
Linotype Syntax™ Bold OsF
Linotype Syntax™ Bold Italic
Linotype Syntax™ Bold Italic OsF
Linotype Syntax™ Heavy
Linotype Syntax™ Heavy OsF
Linotype Syntax™ Heavy Italic

Linotype Syntax™ Heavy Italic OsF
Linotype Syntax™ Black
Linotype Syntax™ Black OsF
Linotype Syntax™ Black Italic
Linotype Syntax™ Black Italic OsF
Linotype Syntax™ Lapidar Text
Regular
Linotype Syntax™ Lapidar Text
Medium
Linotype Syntax™ Lapidar Text
Bold
Linotype Syntax™ Lapidar Text
Heavy
Linotype Syntax™ Lapidar Text
Black
Linotype Syntax™ Lapidar Display
Regular
Linotype Syntax™ Lapidar Display
Medium
Linotype Syntax™ Lapidar Display
Bold
Linotype Syntax™ Lapidar Display
Heavy
Linotype Syntax™ Lapidar Display
Black
Linotype Syntax™ Lapidar Serif
Text Medium
Linotype Syntax™ Lapidar Serif
Text Regular
Linotype Syntax™ Lapidar Serif
Text Bold
Linotype Syntax™ Lapidar Serif
Text Heavy
Linotype Syntax™ Lapidar Serif
Display Regular
Linotype Syntax™ Lapidar Serif
Display Medium
Linotype Syntax™ Lapidar Serif
Display Bold
Linotype Syntax™ Lapidar Serif
Display Heavy
Linotype Syntax™ Letter Light
Linotype Syntax™ Letter Light OsF
Linotype Syntax™ Letter Light
Italic
Linotype Syntax™ Letter Light
Italic OsF
Linotype Syntax™ Letter Regular
Linotype Syntax™ Letter Regular
OsF

Linotype Syntax™ Letter Regular
Italic
Linotype Syntax™ Letter Regular
Italic OsF
Linotype Syntax™ Letter Medium
Linotype Syntax™ Letter Medium
OsF
Linotype Syntax™ Letter Medium
Italic
Linotype Syntax™ Letter Medium
Italic OsF
Linotype Syntax™ Letter Bold
Linotype Syntax™ Letter Bold OsF
Linotype Syntax™ Letter Bold
Italic
Linotype Syntax™ Letter Bold
Italic OsF
Linotype Syntax™ Letter Heavy
Linotype Syntax™ Letter Heavy
OsF
Linotype Syntax™ Letter Heavy
Italic
Linotype Syntax™ Letter Heavy
Italic OsF
Linotype Syntax™ Letter Black
Linotype Syntax™ Letter Black OsF
Linotype Syntax™ Letter Black
Italic
Linotype Syntax™ Letter Black
Italic OsF
Linotype Syntax™ Serif Light
Linotype Syntax™ Serif Light SC
Linotype Syntax™ Serif Light OsF
Linotype Syntax™ Serif Light Italic
Linotype Syntax™ Serif Light Italic
SC
Linotype Syntax™ Serif Light Italic
OsF
Linotype Syntax™ Serif Regular
Linotype Syntax™ Serif Regular SC
Linotype Syntax™ Serif Regular
OsF
Linotype Syntax™ Serif Regular
Italic
Linotype Syntax™ Serif Regular
Italic SC
Linotype Syntax™ Serif Regular
Italic OsF
Linotype Syntax™ Serif Medium
Linotype Syntax™ Serif Medium SC

Linotype Syntax™ Serif Medium
OsF
Linotype Syntax™ Serif Medium
Italic
Linotype Syntax™ Serif Medium
Italic SC
Linotype Syntax™ Serif Medium
Italic OsF
Linotype Syntax™ Serif Bold
Linotype Syntax™ Serif Bold OsF
Linotype Syntax™ Serif Bold Italic
Linotype Syntax™ Serif Bold Italic
OsF
Linotype Syntax™ Serif Heavy
Linotype Syntax™ Serif Heavy OsF
Linotype Syntax™ Serif Heavy
Italic
Linotype Syntax™ Serif Heavy
Italic OsF
Linotype Syntax™ Serif Black
Linotype Syntax™ Serif Black OsF
Linotype Syntax™ Serif Black
Italic
Linotype Syntax™ Serif Black
Italic OsF

Aroma, 1999
Tim Ahrens
Linotype Aroma™ Extra Light
Linotype Aroma™ Extralight Italic
Linotype Aroma™ Light
Linotype Aroma™ SC Light
Linotype Aroma™ Light Italic
Linotype Aroma™ Regular
Linotype Aroma™ SC Regular
Linotype Aroma™ Regular Italic
Linotype Aroma™ Semibold
Linotype Aroma™ SC Semibold
Linotype Aroma™ Semibold Italic
Linotype Aroma™ Bold
Linotype Aroma™ SC Bold
Linotype Aroma™ Bold Italic

Gianotten, 1999
Antonio Pace
Linotype Gianotten™ Light
Linotype Gianotten™ Light Italic
Linotype Gianotten™ Regular
Linotype Gianotten™ Light SC
Linotype Gianotten™ Italic
Linotype Gianotten™ Medium

Linotype Gianotten™ Medium
    Italic
Linotype Gianotten™ Bold
Linotype Gianotten™ Bold Italic
Linotype Gianotten™ Heavy
Linotype Gianotten™ Heavy Italic
Linotype Gianotten™ Black

Milano, 2002
Antonio Pace
Milano™

Markin, 1999
Alfred Tilp
Linotype Markin™ Normal
Linotype Markin™ Normal Italic
Linotype Markin™ Bold
Linotype Markin™ Bold Italic
Linotype Markin™ Ultrabold
Linotype Markin™ Ultrabold Italic

Scarborough, 1998
Akira Kobayashi
ITC Scarborough™ Regular
ITC Scarborough™ Bold

Silvermoon, 1998
Akira Kobayashi
ITC Silvermoon™ Regular
ITC Silvermoon™ Bold

Atomatic, 1997
Johannes Plass
Linotype Atomatic™

Finnegan, 1997
Jürgen Weltin
Linotype Finnegan™ Regular
Linotype Finnegan™ Regular SC
Linotype Finnegan™ Regular OsF
Linotype Finnegan™ Italic
Linotype Finnegan™ Italic SC
Linotype Finnegan™ Italic OsF
Linotype Finnegan™ Medium
Linotype Finnegan™ Medium SC
Linotype Finnegan™ Medium OsF
Linotype Finnegan™ Medium Italic
Linotype Finnegan™ Medium Italic
    SC
Linotype Finnegan™ Medium Italic
    OsF

Linotype Finnegan™ Bold
Linotype Finnegan™ Bold SC
Linotype Finnegan™ Bold OsF
Linotype Finnegan™ Bold Italic
Linotype Finnegan™ Bold Italic SC
Linotype Finnegan™ Bold Italic
    OsF
Linotype Finnegan™ Extra Bold
Linotype Finnegan™ Extra Bold
    OsF
Linotype Finnegan™ Extra Bold
    Italic
Linotype Finnegan™ Extra Bold
    Italic OsF

Spitz, 1997
Oliver Brentzel
Linotype Spitz™ Light
Linotype Spitz™ Book
Linotype Spitz™ Medium
Linotype Spitz™ Bold
Linotype Spitz™ Black

Carumba, 1996
Jill Bell
Carumba™ Plain
Carumba™ Hot Caps

Filosofia, 1996
Zuzana Licko
Filosofia Regular
Filosofia Italic
Filosofia Bold
Filosofia Regular Lining
Filosofia Small Caps
Filosofia All Small Caps
Filosofia Fractions
Filosofia Grand
Filosofia Grand Bold
Filosofia Grand Small Caps
Filosofia Grand All Small Caps
Filosofia Unicase

Tagliatelle, 1996
Alessio Leonardi
F2F Tagliatelle Sugo™

LinoLetter, 1992
Linotype
LinoLetter™ Roman
LinoLetter™ Roman SC

LinoLetter™ Roman OsF
LinoLetter™ Italic
LinoLetter™ Italic OsF
LinoLetter™ Medium
LinoLetter™ Medium SC
LinoLetter™ Medium OsF
LinoLetter™ Medium Italic
LinoLetter™ Medium Italic OsF
LinoLetter™ Bold
LinoLetter™ Bold SC
LinoLetter™ Bold OsF
LinoLetter™ Bold Italic
LinoLetter™ Bold Italic OsF
LinoLetter™ Black
LinoLetter™ Black SC
LinoLetter™ Black OsF
LinoLetter™ Black Italic
LinoLetter™ Black Italic OsF

Didot, 1991
Linotype
Linotype Didot™ Bold
Linotype Didot™ Bold OsF
Linotype Didot™ Headline Roman
Linotype Didot™ Headline Roman
    OsF
Linotype Didot™ Italic
Linotype Didot™ Italic OsF
Linotype Didot™ Medium Initials
Linotype Didot™ Ornaments
Linotype Didot™ Ornaments 1
Linotype Didot™ Ornaments 2
Linotype Didot™ Roman
Linotype Didot™ Roman OsF
Linotype Didot™ Roman SC

Veto, 1994
Marco Ganz
Linotype Veto™ Bold
Linotype Veto™ Bold Italic
Linotype Veto™ Italic
Linotype Veto™ Light
Linotype Veto™ Light Italic
Linotype Veto™ Medium
Linotype Veto™ Medium Italic
Linotype Veto™ Regular

Sho, 1992
Karlgeorg Hoefer
Sho™

Caecilia, 1990
Peter Matthias Noordzij
PMN Caecilia™ 45 Light
PMN Caecilia™ 45 Light OsF
PMN Caecilia™ 45 Light SC
PMN Caecilia™ 46 Light Italic
PMN Caecilia™ 46 Light Italic OsF
PMN Caecilia™ 46 Light Italic SC
PMN Caecilia™ 55 Roman
PMN Caecilia™ 55 Roman OsF
PMN Caecilia™ 55 Roman SC
PMN Caecilia™ 56 Italic
PMN Caecilia™ 56 Italic OsF
PMN Caecilia™ 56 italic SC
PMN Caecilia™ 75 Bold
PMN Caecilia™ 75 Bold OsF
PMN Caecilia™ 75 bold SC
PMN Caecilia™ 76 Bold Italic
PMN Caecilia™ 76 Bold Italic OsF
PMN Caecilia™ 76 Bold Italic SC
PMN Caecilia™ 85 Heavy
PMN Caecilia™ 85 Heavy OsF
PMN Caecilia™ 85 Heavy SC
PMN Caecilia™ 86 Heavy Italic
PMN Caecilia™ 86 Heavy Italic OsF
PMN Caecilia™ 86 Heavy Italic SC
PMN Caecilia™ Central European
    45 Light
PMN Caecilia™ Central European
    46 Light Italic
PMN Caecilia™ Central European
    55 Roman
PMN Caecilia™ Central European
    56 Italic
PMN Caecilia™ Central European
    75 Bold
PMN Caecilia™ Central European
    76 Bold Italic
PMN Caecilia™ Central European
    85 Heavy
PMN Caecilia™ Central European
    86 Heavy Italic

Officina, 1990
Erik Spiekermann
ITC Officina® Sans Bold
ITC Officina® Sans Bold Italic
ITC Officina® Sans Book
ITC Officina® Sans Book Italic
ITC Officina® Serif Bold
ITC Officina® Serif Bold Italic

ITC Officina® Serif Book
ITC Officina® Serif Book Italic

Industria, 1989
Neville Brody
Industria™ Inline
Industria™ Inline Alternate
Industria™ Solid
Industria™ Solid Alternate

Insignia, 1989
Neville Brody
Insignia™
Insignia™ Alternate

Avenir, 1988
Adrian Frutiger
Avenir™ Next Pro Bold
Avenir™ Next Pro Bold Condensed
Avenir™ Next Pro Bold Condensed
    Italic
Avenir™ Next Pro Bold Italic
Avenir™ Next Pro Condensed
Avenir™ Next Pro Condensed Italic
Avenir™ Next Pro Demi
Avenir™ Next Pro Demi Condensed
Avenir™ Next Pro Demi Condensed
    Italic
Avenir™ Next Pro Demi Italic
Avenir™ Next Pro Heavy
Avenir™ Next Pro Heavy
    Condensed
Avenir™ Next Pro Heavy
    Condensed Italic
Avenir™ Next Pro Heavy Italic
Avenir™ Next Pro Italic
Avenir™ Next Pro Medium
Avenir™ Next Pro Medium
    Condensed
Avenir™ Next Pro Medium
    Condensed Italic
Avenir™ Next Pro Medium Italic
Avenir™ Next Pro Regular
Avenir™ Next Pro Ultralight
Avenir™ Next Pro Ultralight
    Condensed
Avenir™ Next Pro Ultralight
    Condensed Italic
Avenir™ Next Pro Ultralight Italic

Frutiger Next, 2001
Adrian Frutiger
Frutiger™ Next Black
Frutiger™ Next Black Italic
Frutiger™ Next Bold
Frutiger™ Next Bold Italic
Frutiger™ Next Central European
    Black
Frutiger™ Next Central European
    Black Condensed
Frutiger™ Next Central European
    Black Italic
Frutiger™ Next Central European
    Bold
Frutiger™ Next Central European
    Bold Condensed
Frutiger™ Next Central European
    Bold Italic
Frutiger™ Next Central European
    Condensed
Frutiger™ Next Central European
    Heavy
Frutiger™ Next Central European
    Heavy Condensed
Frutiger™ Next Central European
    Heavy Italic
Frutiger™ Next Central European
    Italic
Frutiger™ Next Central European
    Light
Frutiger™ Next Central European
    Light Condensed
Frutiger™ Next Central European
    Light Italic
Frutiger™ Next Central European
    Medium
Frutiger™ Next Central European
    Medium Condensed
Frutiger™ Next Central European
    Medium Italic
Frutiger™ Next Central European
    Regular
Frutiger™ Next Condensed Black
Frutiger™ Next Condensed Bold
Frutiger™ Next Condensed Heavy
Frutiger™ Next Condensed Light
Frutiger™ Next Condensed Medium
Frutiger™ Next Condensed Regular
Frutiger™ Next Heavy
Frutiger™ Next Heavy Italic
Frutiger™ Next Italic

Frutiger™ Next Light
Frutiger™ Next Light Italic
Frutiger™ Next Medium
Frutiger™ Next Medium Italic
Frutiger™ Next Regular

Stone, 1987
Sumner Stone
ITC Stone® Informal Bold
ITC Stone® Informal Bold Italic
ITC Stone® Informal Medium
ITC Stone® Informal Medium Italic
ITC Stone® Informal Semi Bold
ITC Stone® Informal Semi Bold
         Italic
ITC Stone® Sans Bold
ITC Stone® Sans Bold Italic
ITC Stone® Sans Medium
ITC Stone® Sans Medium Italic
ITC Stone® Sans Semi Bold
ITC Stone® Sans Semi Bold Italic
ITC Stone® Serif Bold
ITC Stone® Serif Bold Italic
ITC Stone® Serif Medium
ITC Stone® Serif Medium Italic
ITC Stone® Serif Semi Bold
ITC Stone® Serif Semi Bold Italic

Lucida, 1985
Charles Bigelow
Lucida® Sans Bold
Lucida® Sans Bold Italic
Lucida® Sans Italic
Lucida® Sans Roman
Lucida® Serif Bold
Lucida® Serif Bold Italic
Lucida® Serif Italic
Lucida® Serif Roman

Optima nova, 2002
Hermann Zapf
Optima™ nova Black
Optima™ nova Black Italic
Optima™ nova Bold
Optima™ nova Bold Italic
Optima™ nova Bold Italic OsF
Optima™ nova Bold Italic SC
Optima™ nova Bold OsF
Optima™ nova Bold SC
Optima™ nova Condensed Bold
Optima™ nova Condensed Demi

Optima™ nova Condensed Light
Optima™ nova Condensed Medium
Optima™ nova Condensed Regular
Optima™ nova Demi
Optima™ nova Demi Italic
Optima™ nova Demi Italic OsF
Optima™ nova Demi Italic SC
Optima™ nova Demi OsF
Optima™ nova Demi SC
Optima™ nova Heavy
Optima™ nova Heavy Italic
Optima™ nova Italic
Optima™ nova Italic OsF
Optima™ nova Italic SC
Optima™ nova Light
Optima™ nova Light Italic
Optima™ nova Light Italic OsF
Optima™ nova Light Italic SC
Optima™ nova Light OsF
Optima™ nova Light SC
Optima™ nova Medium
Optima™ nova Medium Italic
Optima™ nova Medium Italic OsF
Optima™ nova Medium Italic SC
Optima™ nova Medium OsF
Optima™ nova Medium SC
Optima™ nova Regular
Optima™ nova Regular OsF
Optima™ nova Regular SC
Optima™ nova Titling

Akzidenz Grotesk 1969
Günter Gerhard Lange

Helvetica 1957
Max Miedinger
Helvetica™ Black
Helvetica™ Black Condensed
Helvetica™ Black Condensed
    Oblique
Helvetica™ Black Oblique
Helvetica™ Bold
Helvetica™ Bold Condensed
Helvetica™ Bold Condensed
    Oblique
Helvetica™ Bold Oblique
Helvetica™ Central European Bold
Helvetica™ Central European
    Narrow Bold
Helvetica™ Central European
    Narrow Roman
Helvetica™ Central European
    Roman
Helvetica™ Compressed
Helvetica™ Condensed
Helvetica™ Condensed Oblique
Helvetica™ Cyrillic Bold
Helvetica™ Cyrillic Bold Inclined
Helvetica™ Cyrillic Inclined
Helvetica™ Cyrillic Inserat Upright
Helvetica™ Cyrillic Upright
Helvetica™ Extra Compressed
Helvetica™ Fraction
Helvetica™ Fraction Bold
Helvetica™ Greek Monotonic Bold
Helvetica™ Greek Monotonic Bold
    Inclined
Helvetica™ Greek Monotonic
    Inclined
Helvetica™ Greek Monotonic
    Upright
Helvetica™ Inserat Roman
Helvetica™ Light
Helvetica™ Light Condensed
Helvetica™ Light Condensed
    Oblique
Helvetica™ Light Oblique
Helvetica™ Narrow Bold
Helvetica™ Narrow Bold Oblique
Helvetica™ Narrow Roman
Helvetica™ Narrow Roman Oblique
Helvetica™ Roman

Helvetica™ Roman Oblique
Helvetica™ Rounded Black
Helvetica™ Rounded Black Oblique
Helvetica™ Rounded Bold
Helvetica™ Rounded Bold
    Condensed
Helvetica™ Rounded Bold
    Condensed Oblique
Helvetica™ Rounded Bold Oblique
Helvetica™ Textbook Bold
Helvetica™ Textbook Bold Oblique
Helvetica™ Textbook Roman
Helvetica™ Textbook Roman
    Oblique
Helvetica™ Ultra Compressed

Futura 1932
Paul Renner
Futura® Black
Futura® Bold
Futura® Bold Condensed
Futura® Bold Condensed Oblique
Futura® Bold Oblique
Futura® Book
Futura® Book Oblique
Futura® Central European Bold
Futura® Central European Bold
    Condensed
Futura® Central European Bold
    Oblique
Futura® Central European Book
Futura® Central European Book
    Oblique
Futura® Central European Extra
    Bold
Futura® Central European Extra
    Bold Oblique
Futura® Central European Heavy
Futura® Central European Heavy
    Oblique
Futura® Central European Light
Futura® Central European Light
    Oblique
Futura® Central European Medium
Futura® Central European Medium
    Oblique
Futura® Display
Futura® Extra Bold
Futura® Extra Bold Condensed
Futura® Extra Bold Condensed
    Oblique

Futura® Extra Bold Oblique
Futura® Extra Bold Shaded
Futura® Headline Black
Futura® Headline Display
Futura® Headline Extra Bold
    Shaded
Futura® Headline Script
Futura® Heavy
Futura® Heavy Oblique
Futura® Light
Futura® Light Condensed
Futura® Light Condensed Oblique
Futura® Light Oblique
Futura® Medium
Futura® Medium Condensed
Futura® Medium Condensed
    Oblique
Futura® Medium Oblique
Futura® Script

Gill Sans 1928–30
Eric Gill
Gill Sans® Bold
Gill Sans® Bold Condensed
Gill Sans® Bold Italic
Gill Sans® Central European Bold
Gill Sans® Central European Bold
    Italic
Gill Sans® Central European Italic
Gill Sans® Central European Light
Gill Sans® Central European Light
    Italic
Gill Sans® Central European Roman
Gill Sans® Condensed
Gill Sans® Display Extra Bold
Gill Sans® Extra Bold
Gill Sans® Extra Condensed Bold
Gill Sans® Italic
Gill Sans® Light
Gill Sans® Light Italic
Gill Sans® Light Shadowed
Gill Sans® Roman
Gill Sans® Shadowed
Gill Sans® Ultra Bold
Gill Sans® Ultra Bold Condensed

Times New Roman 1832
Stanley Morison
Times New Roman™ Bold
Times New Roman™ Bold
    Condensed

Times New Roman™ Bold Italic
Times New Roman™ Condensed
Times New Roman™ Condensed
                    Italic
Times New Roman™ Italic
Times New Roman™ Roman

Bodoni 1790
Giambattista Bodoni
Bodoni Bold
Bodoni Bold Condensed
Bodoni Bold Italic
Bodoni Book
Bodoni Book Italic
Bodoni Italic
Bodoni Roman

Baskerville 1754
John Baskerville
Baskerville™ Bold
Baskerville™ Medium
Baskerville™ Medium Italic
Baskerville™ Regular
Baskerville™ Regular Italic
Baskerville™ Regular Old Face

Caslon 1725
William Caslon
Caslon #3 Italic
Caslon #3 Italic OsF
Caslon #3 Roman
Caslon #3 Roman SC
Caslon 540 Italic
Caslon 540 Italic OsF
Caslon 540 Roman
Caslon 540 Roman SC

Stempel Garamond 1543
Claude Garamond
Stempel Garamond™ Bold
Stempel Garamond™ Bold Italic
Stempel Garamond™ Bold Italic
                    OsF
Stempel Garamond™ Bold OsF
Stempel Garamond™ Italic
Stempel Garamond™ Italic OsF
Stempel Garamond™ Roman
Stempel Garamond™ Roman OsF
Stempel Garamond™ Roman SC

398

www.adobe.com

www.buymyfonts.com

www.bertholdtypes.com

www.bitstream.com

www.identifont.com

www.chank.com

www.devicefonts.co.uk

www.dutchtypelibrary.nl

www.emigre.com/fonts

www.fontbureau.com

www.fonts.com

www.fontshop.com

www.fontsmith.com

www.gerardunger.com

www.houseind.com

www.letterror.com

www.linotype.com

www.lucasfonts.com

www.teff.nl

www.typedesign.com

www.typefonderie.com

www.typography.com

www.typography.net

www.stormtype.com

www.t26.com

www.underware.com

www.virusfonts.com

www.hollandfonts.com

Cees W. de Jong
Designer and publisher born in 1945
in Amsterdam. He graduated from the
Gerrit Rietveld Academy in 1970. From
1975 until 2004, he was director of
V+K Design-Publishing, a design studio
and publishing company specializing
in international books on design and
architecture, a number of which have
received awards. He now works as a
design consultant.

Alston W. Purvis
Professor of the visual arts division of
the School of Arts at Boston University,
USA. Author of many books on design,
for example, *Dutch Graphic Design,
1918-1945*, *Wendingen*, *A Century of
Posters* and *Graphic Design 20th Century*.

Friedrich Friedl
Professor of typography at the Academy
of Design, Offenbach am Main. His
work has been exhibited widely and
he is author of many books on
typography and design and numerous
articles for magazines.

Design
Cees W. de Jong, V K Projects

Layout and DTP
Cees W. de Jong, V K Projects
Pascal van den Dungen, FritzRepro

Translated from the Dutch by
Roz Vatter-Buck, Doe-Eye

Illustrations, drawings, photographs
and fonts supplied by Friedrich Friedl,
Gerard Unger, Hermann Zapf, Erik van
Blokland, Jean François Porchez, Hans
Eduard Meier, Tim Ahrens, Antonio
Pace, Alfred Tilp, Akira Kobayashi,
Johannes Plass, Jürgen Weltin, Oliver
Brentzel, Jill Bell, Zuzana Licko,
Alessio Leonardi, Marco Ganz, Karlgeorg
Hoefer, David Berlow, Peter Matthias
Noordzij, Erik Spiekermann, Neville
Brody, Adrian Frutiger, Sumner Stone,
Charles Bigelow, Kris Holmes, Linotype
Library Gmbh, Otmar Hoefer, Cees de
Jong, V K Projects, Martijn Le Coultre.

Every care has been taken in properly
crediting the reproductions in this
publication.

First published in the United Kingdom
in 2005 by
Thames & Hudson Ltd
181A High Holborn
London WC1V 7QX

www.thamesandhudson.com

© 2005 Thames & Hudson Ltd, London

Original edition © 2005 V K Projects

British Library Cataloguing-in-
Publication Data
A catalogue record for this book is
available from the British Library

ISBN-13: 978-0-500-51229-6
ISBN-10: 0-500-51229-9

Printed and bound in Singapore

The end, with Z for Zapfino